GENERATIVE COACHING

Volume 2

Enriching the Steps of Creative and Sustainable Change

International Association for Generative Change

114 Ponderosa Drive

Santa Cruz, CA 95060

USA

E-Mail: info@generative-change.com

Homepage: https://generative-change.com/

Library of Congress Control Number: 2021907725

I.S.B.N. 978-0-578-35913-7

GENERATIVE COACHING

Volume 2

Enriching the Steps of Creative and Sustainable Change

Stephen Gilligan

Robert B. Dilts

Design and illustrations: Antonio Meza

TABLE OF CONTENTS

TABLE OF CONTENTS

TABLE OF CONTENTS

Generative Coaching

Dedication

We dedicate this volume to the many people and communities that inspired us to live life with creativity and love.

For Steve, a few examples are his mother, his Italian grandfather, many great teachers, the many people who should have given up and didn't, and countless artists and transformational leaders.

For Robert, a few examples are his parents Patricia and Robert, his children Andrew and Julia, his brothers Michael, Daniel and John, his sister Mary and his wife Deborah. In addition, there are the "giants" upon whose shoulders he stands, many of whom he has written about in his books.

For each of us, we are on the lookout in every interaction for examples of this creative light. Especially now, we need to notice them every day.

Acknowledgments

We would like to gratefully acknowledge all of those who have helped and supported us to bring our generative coaching work into the world. This includes the sponsors, colleagues and students who have participated in helping us develop this work. Particular gratitude goes to those who participated in the demonstrations presented in this volume.

We also want to acknowledge all of the members of the International Association for Generative Change who have joined us in brining this dream to a reality including our fellow teachers, professional members, associate members and other participants in the IAGC community who are as passionate about the work as we are.

We give special thanks to Susanne Kessler who both transcribed and proofread the materials that make up these pages, elegantly integrating the roles of Realist and Positive Critic.

We are deeply grateful to our illustrator Antonio Meza who did the amazing artwork for this volume. We continue to be astonished and impressed with Antonio's versatility and his genius in visually capturing not only our message but the spirit of Generative Change from which it comes. As with *Generative Coaching Volume 1*, Antonio's drawings bring the work alive in ways that our words could not possibly accomplish.

Steve and Robert

Preface

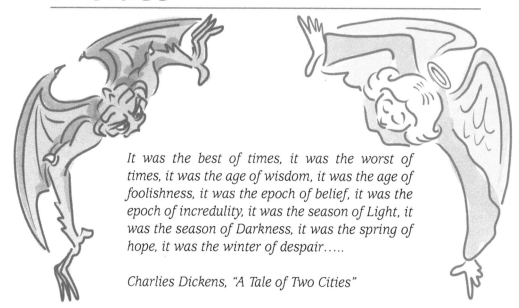

It was the best of times, it was the worst of times, it was the age of wisdom, it was the age of foolishness, it was the epoch of belief, it was the epoch of incredulity, it was the season of Light, it was the season of Darkness, it was the spring of hope, it was the winter of despair…..

Charlies Dickens, "A Tale of Two Cities"

While written about the times around the French Revolution, surely these words equally describe our present situation. The old institutions are rapidly fading, our environment is hanging by a thread, and the way forward is not clear. The two Chinese characters for "crisis"—danger and opportunity — seem emblazoned across the sky.

The dangers are ominous and escalating—ever-increasing ego-isolation, fascism, loss of trust and shared vision, impotent governments. But enhanced opportunity also is growing—new communities and consciousness are sprouting in countless ways. Sometimes it seems like the forces of destruction and creative love are in a race to some epochal point, the outcome unknown and unknowable.

Such extraordinary times call out for new ways of thinking, acting, relating, and being. This is our purpose in developing generative coaching—to be part of the growing collective of new ways to create reality. We have known each other for over 45 years, our lives and professional paths intersecting repeatedly, with a shared vision and complementary skills/approaches. Generative coaching emerged from this partnership, as a "coach" or vehicule to allow deeper connection to life, to support the creation of worlds to which we can all belong.

Our collaboration led us to develop a 15-day certification program that is offered in many places across the world. The model is a description of how consciousness creates reality, both negative and

positive versions, and how we can align with that consciousness to transform negativity and create positive realities. We usually teach it in four modules, each module deepening a framework that includes core principles, the six steps, multiple methods/techniques for each step, and perhaps most importantly, a way of organizing the creative state to potentiate these creative processes. We emphasize the state of the coach as much as the state of the client, and give even deeper emphasis to the relational state that creative systems share.

This is the second of the four volumes of the generative coaching approach. It builds on volume 1, providing a deeper and more elaborated process for doing the work. In the certification program, we usually do a joint presentation of the first and fourth modules, with solo modules in between. So volumes 1 and 4 are our joint voices, while this volume is Steve's voice, and volume 3 is Robert's. Whether presenting jointly or solo, we are, in the words of our teacher, Dr. Milton Erickson, "a part of yet apart from" each other. For us, this is one of the strengths of generative coaching: it illuminates how each person has their own unique voice and contribution, while the collaboration of those unique voices opens possibilities we never imagined. This is our commitment to each other, and to the world in general. The world needs such creative partnerships more than ever, and we hope this work supports them in all living beings.

Steve Gilligan and Robert Dilts

Chapter 1

Overview of Generative Coaching

Background and Beginnings

The Buddhists like to say that when you have been given a human life, you are so lucky. Infinite possibilities for living a creative and happy life! There's another saying that the more you practice, the luckier you get! Generative Coaching is a way to practice creativity so that we're lucky enough to create worlds to which we all want to belong. In this first chapter, we overview the core premises of Generative Coaching, as a platform upon which we can understand and intelligently practice the work.

The core premises can be simply described as:

1. Reality is constructed

2. Through conversations

3. Moving through filters

4. Held with either open or closed presence.

Let's take a look at what these premises mean...

Premise 1: Reality is Constructed

Generative Coaching is about creativity and how to coach creativity. We see creativity as not something that a few brilliant people do occasionally, but as the heart and soul of all human experience. It is not a "thing" located inside of a fixed space, but an ever-changing emergence that arises from conversations and connections between differences. This idea of creativity as conversation has been around for a long time, as this 16th century poem from Kabir illuminates:

Between the conscious and the unconscious, the mind has put up a swing: all earth creatures, even the supernovas, sway between these two trees, and it never winds down.

Angels, animals, humans, insects by the million, also the wheeling sun and moon; ages go by, and it goes on.

Everything is swinging: heaven, earth, water, fire, and the secret one slowly growing a body.

Kabir saw that for fifteen seconds, and it made him a servant for life.

– Kabir (English version by Robert Bly)

So may we see that for at least fifteen seconds.

When we say that reality is created in each moment, we don't mean that each moment is generative: Most of the time, reality is automatically re-generated from conditioned "default values." That is, unless you bring mindful human presence, you mostly repeat the past. This gives the illusory feeling that reality is just happening independently, that it's something "out there" that we are not participating in creating. Most of the time we are just living in habituated conditioning. And some of the conditioning may be in very large systems – for example, we live in centuries old patterns of racism and misogyny – and it feels like it's just the way life always is.

But in Generative Coaching we see that things are not so fixed or static: everything is impermanent and forever changing. We see this, for example, in the hyper-speed of technological change: We live in a world today that was unimaginable even 20 years ago. My daughter, who is 29, has never seen a typewriter. When I was in Graduate School in the late 70s, every professor in the Psychology Department had two secretaries, one totally devoted to typing on an IBM typewriter – eight hours a day. I did my dissertation on a word processor that could contain a *whole chapter* – thirty pages, double spaced – on one floppy disk! Amazing! A very different reality has been created since then.

This idea that consciousness creates reality can also be seen in the well-known *placebo effect*, which is why today most basic research in medicine requires double blind tests. The term 'placebo' is Latin for "I please" – which means people will produce results consistent with beliefs and expectations, regardless of the "real" condition. So, if I believe I'm being given a psychoactive drug to cure my depression, but really only given a sugar pill, my depression relief is about the same as when I took the "real thing."

So, our consciousness is primary in creating the reality in which we find ourselves. The common and deepest ingredient in both the negative and positive parts of your life is *you*. Your connection to the consciousness that creates the world is the difference that makes the difference. We don't say this to blame you—*oh great, not only does my life suck, but it's all my fault*—but rather to empower. Every moment contains potential heavens and hells: it's your relationship to it that decides.

You didn't have this capacity when you were young, and most of us have been so deeply conditioned to not know our own creative power. Generative Coaching is a way to align with creative consciousness to generate positive realities for you and your communities. It is not an ego power to control and dominate others—that illusion is at the heart of impotence and misery—but an integral consciousness that allows you to feel a belonging and interconnectedness to the world.

We will say so much more about this. For now, we emphasize that everything we know as reality, we are actively participating in creating it. So, if you don't like the reality that you're experiencing, then change it. That's really a central focus in Generative Coaching.

Premise 2: Reality is Created through Conversations

This reality construction happens through conversations—not just human conversations, but exchanges everywhere in the universe—the sun and the moon, the connections that hold galaxies and solar systems together, the conversations between verbal and nonverbal intelligences, between mothers and infants. Everything is pulsating, communicating, interconnecting – that's the true nature of reality. If we can feel aligned and in the creative flow of these conversations, good things happen; but when information-energy flow stops or is blocked, creativity stops. So creativity does not come from a position, a state, a belief – rather it is this movement of information-energy through many different positions. For Generative Coaching, we focus on three types of conversational creativity:

1. The classical/quantum (or realist/dreamer) conversation

2. The cognitive/somatic conversation

3. The self/other(s) conversation

1. **Classical/quantum.** Reality is created through a movement between the infinite potential of the creative imagination and the specific actualities of the classical world. Each completes the other. Without the openness and freedom of the quantum ocean, there can't be much creativity, yet the infinity of the quantum field also needs to be in conversation with the classical world. We find this in the still central four-step creativity model proposed about 100 years ago by Graham Wallas (Wallas 1926).

Four-step Model of Creativity:
The Conversation between the Worlds

2. INCUBATION
Rest period ("no mind")
(creative unconscious)

1. PREPARATION
Intense focus and effort on
goal (conscious mind)

3. ILLUMINATION
"Light bulb goes off: Aha!!"
(creative unconscious)

**4. TRANSLATION INTO
REALITY:**
Hard work to make it real
(conscious mind)

According to this model you first have a *preparation phase*, in which you need a focus, commitment or question, and hard work. When you sense diminishing returns, you back off and take a break, which is the so-called *incubation phase*. Here you let go and open to a solution. Then hopefully a new idea, an *illumination* comes from someplace else. And last, you have to **translate it into action** in the fourth phase, in which the conscious mind is again more active.

For me, for example, many generative insights have occurred in my California hot tub. I may be working all day on a project at my desk- that's the first step – but around midnight, I go into the backyard and sit in the hot tub. Many times, the tension dissolves into the mists – that's the second step – and then, on a lucky night, some lucid beautiful awareness arises. (Illumination!!). Then, as we say in English, the devil is in the details: That lucid insight has to be translated into reality through deep commitment and hard work.

Thus, creativity is a rhythm between conscious intention and unconscious "dreaming." To surf this "middle way," we need a balanced state of *not too tight, not too loose* . Or as the saying goes in card playing, *you have to know when to hold them, and when to fold them.* When to follow your map, and when to release it to dip back into the creative ocean and fish for new ones. Creativity is the art of surfing that middle way: It's in the conversation between the realist world and the great infinite ocean of imagination. The Chinese call this **wu-wei**; we call it generative consciousness.

2. The cognitive/somatic conversation.

Another core conversation is between the cognitive and the somatic. Whenever generativity is needed, the mind and body (and much more!) need to be connected. Our teacher Gregory Bateson often quoted Pascal:

> *The heart has its reasons which reason knows nothing of...*
> *We know the truth not only by the reason, but by the heart.*
> *We feel it in a thousand things.*

The old traditional "disembodied intellect" model of cognition has been supplanted in cognitive science by what is called the "4 E model" (see Damasio, 1994; Varela, Thompson, and Rosch, 1991) that emphasizes cognition as:

1. Embodied

2. Embedded (in contexts or fields: the environment, the cultural, the social context, etc.)

3. Expressive (musicality, somatic movements, etc.)

4. Enactive (connected to actions)

In other words, thinking is a multi-modal field that interconnects ideas with bodies, relationships, actions, movement, and multiple contexts. For an idea to be generative, it must have positive connections to each of these.

In terms of the "head-body" conversation—what we call the vertical axis—a general question used frequently in generative coaching is:

As you say (or think or hear) that, what do you notice happening in your body?

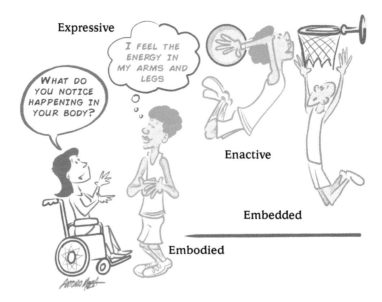

This "vertical axis" is crucial if an idea is to be generative.

Unfortunately, mainstream traditions generally teach an adversarial dominance/submission relationship between the verbal and somatic minds. This *"mind over body"* stance produces an isolated ego at the root of persistent problems and suffering. To move to a generative level, we're looking to integrate the verbal mind into a mutually respectful conversation with other cognitive dimensions.

3. The self/other conversation. In our generative cognition model, consciousness and creativity is not located inside of a single person or group or tradition. It emerges from conversations between our "self" position and the multiple, even contradictory "other" positions or truths. This "other" has many forms: another person, a conflicting view within one's self, another gender or culture, a social adversary, one's intimacy partner, and so on. There is no shortage of truths or realities "other than" our ego position. When we identify only with our "ego self" position, problems and symptoms result. Thus, at the heart of generative change is welcoming conflicting relationships into a conversational field where each position is valued and given place. Over and over, we see how when this occurs, transformational creativity results.

Premise 3: Reality is Constructed through Filters

These "consciousness conversations" are mediated through *filters* – like light striking a prism, or the sun shining through the stained-glass windows in a beautiful cathedral. You can see this in the Gaudí cathedral in Barcelona, the 'Sagrada Familia". Sunlight streams through windows, creating a sacred feeling of being inside a divine home. The stained-glass windows are a metaphorical example of a filter: they translate the river of consciousness into specific forms. There are countless filters simultaneously operating: your somatic state; your beliefs and intention; your personal history, family, and culture; the social, environmental, and political contexts.

This is what psychology studies: how experience and behavior is mediated through the many filters that distinguish an identity state. At a basic level, experiences like color, emotion, freedom, separate objects, etc. are not "out there" in the world; they are actively created by our nervous systems.

Humans have exceptional freedom to set their filters in infinitely possible ways, resulting in many different realities. For example, kindness has 10,000 different faces, each expressing a different reality. The same is true for virtually every other human distinction: trust, success, "my child," "my body," fierceness, etc. Each can be represented in countless ways, each way a filter through which a different reality emerges. Each filter takes a deep structure or archetypal pattern that contains many possible maps and translates into one particular reality. In a significant way, you become what you imagine as real.

As such, we give much attention to which filters are in play. We're identifying which filters are being used to create a *"stuck state,"* and which might allow a more generative outcome.

Unchanging realities represent fixed filters. The limits are not in the world, they are in the filters used to create a world. Some filters may be individual, many are collective, most are unconscious and automatic (i.e., conditioned). They may be centuries-old traditions or beliefs, or long-standing transgenerational cultural or family patterns, or gender/racial stereotypes. Regardless, stuck states reflect fixed filters. To support creative change, we need to identify the limiting filters, then open a conversational space to loosen their grip and allow an intelligent reconfiguration of these representational maps.

creating reality

In Generative Coaching we look at three types of filters:

1. Somatic, cognitive, and field minds

2. Individual representational maps (beliefs, emotions, images, etc.)

3. Performance holons

cognitive mind

somatic mind

field mind

1. Somatic, Cognitive, and Field Minds

In *GC1 (Generative Coaching, Volume 1)*, we identified three main types of "minds" or intelligences: Somatic, Cognitive, and Field. This *"triunal consciousness"* model means that our reality is created through conversations between these three general modalities. Thus, generative coaching gives equal focus to each general filter: How experience is being represented in the verbal social mind, how it is represented in the embodied somatic mind, and how it is represented in the multiple contexts at play. In problem areas, there is inevitably incongruence within and between these modalities. The verbal mind might be thinking one thing, while the somatic mind is thinking another; or the field mind might contain "critical voices" or threatening presences that severely constrain individual experience; or perhaps there are conflicting intentions such as, *I want to be open, but I need to preserve my boundaries.* For sustainable change, these different and often-conflicting representations need to be welcomed and integrated into a generative self. We gave significant attention to this challenge in Volume 1, and we will continue this emphasis in the present volume.

2. Single representational maps

Each of the three minds has many different "parts" or dimensions. For example, cognitive consciousness carries representations such as belief, intention, meaning, plans, and many other kinds of values. Somatic consciousness includes posture, breathing, movement, rhythm, level of tension, actions, emotions, and so forth. And field consciousness can include physical environment, social context, historical fields, different people and places, etc.

So, while we use the three minds (somatic, cognitive, and field) as a sort of middle-level coaching structure, we also need to "chunk down" into more specific levels such as: What specific belief is being used, and how can it be modified? What underlying emotion is present, and how can it become fluid? What "invisible field presences" are active--historical resources, critical parents from childhood, resources--that can be positively engaged in the creative process? We coach a person to find a generative state within each of the minds, then help them adjust those individual maps (beliefs, somatic state, resources, etc.) to optimize their performance. The core idea: Each individual map can be represented in infinite possible ways, and a generative state allows the fluid adjustment of each map to meet (what Milton Erickson described as) *the ever-shifting needs and challenges of the present moment*. To do that effectively, we need to be able to sift through the many possible "small chunk" maps in play, and know how to update and upgrade them into the generative state needed for success.

In the field : my grandfather

I DESERVE THIS

In my mind : an empowering belief

In my body : morning walk

3. Performance Holons: The prototype filter for Generative Coaching

In emphasizing creativity as central to human being – that is, we actively participate in creating virtually every level of our reality – we are challenged to identify how this happens. My Stanford mentor Karl Pribram (1971) coined the term images of achievement to describe this process by which we map where we are, where we want to be, what are the best ways of getting there, how to deal with the inevitable challenges, etc. These "performance maps" are the "action strategies" through which we create our lives, the "operating manuals" we use to construct realities. Because human consciousness prefers an underlying sense of unity, these "performance maps" are not linear or separate bits and pieces; they integrate our understandings and values in a multi-dimensional map we call a performance holon. We consider these performance holons as the prototype filters for generative change work.

The term *holon* was proposed by Arthur Koestler (1965) to describe a creative system of interconnected parts. Each part is its own self-organizing whole, that contains its own parts... all the way down. A human relationship is an obvious example of a holon: If we have a relationship, that's its own unity; but it contains "you" and "me" as self-organizing wholes. The same is true for any team—business, family, sports—or for a musical orchestra, or a complex eco-system. *Holon* is a beautiful idea for recognizing the part/whole identity of intelligent life forms: I am whole as "me," but part as "we." Each level has its own creative properties, so being able to move between the levels enables much deeper creativity.

And we use the term *performance* to emphasize that these maps are used especially to *perform* a creative act: for example, to create a successful outcome at work; to create a positive body; to create a positive social community; and so forth. We emphasize that life is best regarded as a performance art, as an act of creativity; and that generative coaching should be similarly regarded. The performance holons are the representations by which this creative life happens.

The core performance holon in generative change work has six dimensions:

1. Desired state (goal/intention/value/mission/etc.)

2. Present state

3. Achievement maps ("how")

4. Resources

5. Obstacles

6. Underlying context (COACH vs. CRASH)

Creative Performance HOLON

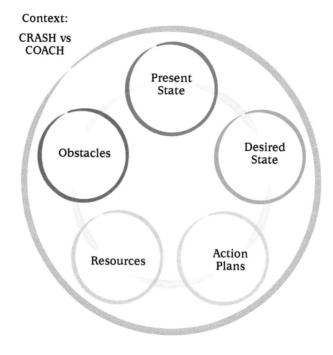

At a basic level, this holon provides the 6-step model central to Generative Coaching:

1. Open a COACH field

2. Set a positive intention

3. Develop a generative state

4. Take action

5. Transform obstacles

6. Post-session practice

This was the primary focus of Volume 1. These six steps provide a basic structure for modeling a client's identity patterns. As is shown in the Appendices, we use them for a pre-session assessment (Appendix B), as well as post-session feedback and assessment (Appendix D). In fact, we contend that the "differences that make a difference" in a coaching session can be seen by comparing the two forms. That is, we propose that significant changes in these six steps will reflect significant session-related changes.

At a next level, we can see the performance holon as a mandala-like map:

Generative Holons: Each part is valued, interconnected, held in fluid forms

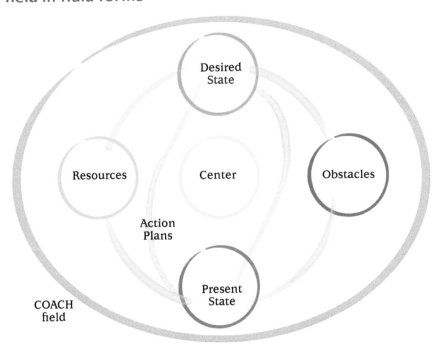

This allows us to see the interconnected nature of the parts: (1) the present state and desired state are a complementary pair, and (2) the resources and obstacles are a second pair. A fifth dimension is the "action plans" that move on a timeline between present state and desired state. The final dimension is the meta-level distinction of whether these core dimensions are being held in the *creative flow* of a COACH field, which allows generative relationships; or a CRASH field, which locks the parts in a rigid, non-collaborative state.

At this more advanced level, which is the primary focus of this second volume, each step contains the others. They are not so much separate, linear steps, but different dimensions of an integrated system of sustainable change. At any point in a session when the process seems unclear or muddled, we can quickly check whether we have well-formed maps of each part of the holon. It usually reveals that some part is not fully present in the conversation and orients us to where the conversation needs attention.

Such questions might include:

* *What level of COACH state is there right now? What are the resource connections to COACH?*

* *What is the intention/goal? How much motivation? How resonant is it?*

* *What resources are here? Are they sufficient to keep a stable COACH state?*

* *Is there a sense of what actions to take?*

* *What obstacles are present? Are there hidden obstacles in the field? What are the signs that a person is disconnecting?*

Coaching with the performance holon allows such questions to always be in the background, providing ways to sense and skillfully respond to the most subtle signs of disconnection or CRASH. For example, a conversation about how to reach a goal might start feeling "muddy" or discordant, like out-of-tune music. A quick use of the above questions might indicate, for example, that some obstacle has just activated in mid-sentence, evidenced by muscle tension and a loss of resonance. The coach would thus shift attention to resources or somatic centering, ensuring a balanced state is rediscovered before focusing further on the goal. Thus, generative coaching seeks to develop and maintain a field where all the different elements—present and desired state, resources, and obstacles, etc.—are in balance. We are coaching wholeness and integral consciousness: This is what produces sustainable change.

Premise 4: Each Experiential Reality is held with Open (COACH) or Locked (CRASH) Presence

Now we come to the most important distinction in generative coaching: the state in which a performance occurs. In Volume 1, we described two core states: the creative generativity of a COACH state vs. the neuro-muscularly locked problem state of CRASH. Let's review these distinctions briefly here.

To understand what we mean by a COACH state, let's consider human performance at its finest. Think of a great athlete, musician, artist, or leader; or a championship team, great orchestra, or creative community; or when you are in a beautiful nature environment or feeling love with your beloved. What do all these have in common? How do you feel when you observe or participate in them? What words would you use to describe them?

The acronym *COACH* identifies some of the basic dimensions of that state. We feel:

Centered

Open

Aware

Connected

Hospitable

The COACH State : Integrated Holon

    COACH is a state of what the Chinese call "double happiness": (1) you feel great! and (2) you do your best work. Thus, COACH is the ground for positive living, and a primary responsibility of the generative coach is to activate and then maintain the "disciplined flow" of a COACH state, in both clients and one's self.

In terms of the performance holon, COACH is the experience of an integrated, generative holon. In this state, all parts of the creative "team" are positive contributors:)

Characteristics of a Creative Performance System (COACH Holon)

1. Underlying "field" context: Limbic resonance, musicality, curiosity, feedback, and feed-forward

2. Each part is welcomed

3. Each part is positively valued

4. Each part's maps are fluid and context sensitive: Infinite forms, content, meanings.

5. All parts are inter-connected and æsthetically balanced

6. Actions of part/whole are guided by æsthetic resonance

7. "Mandala-like": center, unified field, balanced pairs of opposites

Thus, we operate from the principle:

Before you ask your clients (or yourself) to engage in a challenging task, create conditions for success by activating a COACH state.

It's one thing to activate a COACH state, it's another to maintain it. In fact, most people can find a COACH state under positive circumstances—a space of no stress, where everything is pleasant and easy—but not when stressful situations occur. If so, COACH states become a type of positive dissociation, a way to avoid what Shakespeare called "the valences and vicissitudes" of ordinary living.

So, while we use positive reference structures in accessing a COACH state—for example, revivifying a transcendent, peaceful feeling in nature—the real benefit comes from activating COACH in troubling experiences – a relationship problem, or job crisis, or health issue. This is what makes COACH so valuable.

The "evil twin" of COACH is CRASH:

Contracted

Reactive

Analysis Paralysis

Separated

Hostile/ Hurting/ Hating

The CRASH State : Disconnected from the Whole

Here our consciousness is imprisoned in *neuromuscular lock*, expressed in the "four F's" of *fight*, *flight*, *freeze*, or *fold*. Our consciousness becomes saturated with negative anger, fear, disconnected thinking, or "giving up" (depression, drugs/alcohol, TV). In this toxic state, you're cut off from yourself, your resources, your creative imagination. All you can do is rearrange the chairs on the Titanic, there's no way out.

In terms of the performance holon, in CRASH at least some parts of your experience are regarded and experienced as negative; you are a "fundamentalist" who can't move through multiple representations of a map; you can't directly feel your body; it doesn't feel like the world is safe and full of resources.

Patterns of a CRASH holon

1. Underlying field context: CRASH (anger/fear/ disembodied/depressed

2. Some parts are not welcome or recognized

3. Some parts are negatively valued ("bad")

4. "Fundamentalism": maps are rigid and feedback-unresponsive (surface content, forms, meanings)

5. Functional isolation ("dissociation") of parts

6. Parts are in "zero sum" competition

7. No systemic integrity: no center; no unified field, imbalanced and fragmented relationships

What we're saying is that the exact same situation can become either a tremendously positive event or a horribly negative experience, *depending on the state in which you hold it*. Let's imagine, for example, that you grew up in a very difficult family and were going home for the holidays. If you approach it in a CRASH state—tensing up when you imagine it, "knowing" it will be a disaster, meeting your family member(s) in an anxious and angry state, getting easily triggered into old negative patterns, anticipating the worse is still to come—this would undoubtedly create the nightmare event you dreaded most. And adding insult to injury, you would blame it all on yourself and/or them, digging the hole of disconnected misery deeper, setting up the next negative experience.

Now let's imagine you approach that same situation in COACH. You find a connection with yourself deeper than the family pain; you practice how to connect to that positive state when triggered; you give first attention to your COACH state during the visit; you creatively engage with the stuck points; and so on. Clearly, this would produce a profoundly different experience, in you and (maybe) the others as well.

CRASH as "neuromuscular lock": Maps get fixed/frozen

Fight   Freeze

Flight   Fold

So we think of COACH and CRASH as not just surface states of "positive vs. negative" content, but as a deeper consciousness that opens to, or dissociates from, each unique moment, thereby creating either solutions or problems. A COACH state doesn't mean just thinking positive thoughts or smiling or having only pleasant experiences; it is a deeper presence that holds both suffering and joy with equal creative connection. It doesn't avoid the difficulties of life; it opens to and through them, in a way that humanizes and integrates life.

This power is within each of us. When we realize it, our dreams can become realities, we can find the best in ourselves and others, we can create a world to which we want to belong. This is why we consider COACH as the core meta-distinction of the work. Now, as we move to elaborate each of the six steps of Generative Coaching that we covered in the first module, we hope you can appreciate deeper how it is the difference that makes the difference.

Summary

In Generative Coaching, we operate from the premise that reality is created by consciousness, and we are active participants in this process. This creative process involves "conversations," such as between the quantum "dreamer" consciousness and the "realist" worldly consciousness, as well as more local conversations between the verbal (cognitive) and nonverbal (somatic) minds, and the "self" position and the many "others" in the identity field. These conversations use filters or *representational* maps to translate fields of creative potential into specific realities.

Each pattern has equal capacity to be destructive or constructive, depending on how we use it. So even more important than the pattern or map is the human presence using it. COACH is a creative state that supports positive and transformative realities, whereas CRASH is a destructive force. So in coaching, we're connecting clients to their deepest positive intention, then supporting them to find their best creative state to realize that dream.

To put all this into action, we return to the 6-step model that was the framework for Volume 1, this time exploring more advanced applications for each step. May the journey support you in being the person you most want to be, and help you to create the communities you most want to live in.

There was a Japanese Zen master named Nan-in who lived during the Meiji era (1868-1912). During his days as a teacher, he was visited by a university professor curious about Zen. Being polite, Nan-in served the professor a cup of tea.

As he poured, the professor's cup became full, but Nan-in kept on pouring. As the professor watched the cup overflow, he could no longer contain himself and said, "It is overfull. No more will go in!"

Nan-in turned to the professor and said, "Like the cup, you are too full of your own opinions and speculations. How can I show you Zen unless you first empty your cup?

Chapter 2

Step 1
Opening the COACH field

The starting point for all creative action is to first empty the mind, and reconnect with a deep presence within one's self and within the world as a whole. In doing so, our thoughts and actions can be clear and authentic, springing from a deep mysterious pool. This is a prerequisite for developing sustainable positive changes.

This is not a mechanical, linear process, but part of a natural conversation. Thus, a typical first part of a session might begin with a few minutes of "social chit-chat", and then move to an informal description of the session goal:

> *Take a few minutes and tell me about what you most want to achieve today.*

As the client talks, the coach begins to settle into a COACH state, opening a deep, centered listening space.

From there, the coach can invite the client to do the same:

> *It sounds like you really have an important goal and challenge, and I'd love to support you in achieving it. To do that, I think a good first step is to connect to the very best of who you are.*

Most clients agree that it would be great to do this, but don't know if and how it's possible. This is a first place where the generative coach earns his or her keep: by helping the client develop a sustainable *COACH field*.

In the first volume, we talked about two methods by which this can be done. The first was guiding clients through a simple **C**(enter)- **O**(pen) – **A**(ware) – **C**(onnect to center/intention/field)– **H**(ospitable welcoming of whatever comes). The coach uses the 3 Rs of **rhythm, resonance, and repetition** to ensure a creative effect.

The second method, which we call the **Step 1 prototype,** is revivifying COACH-like experiences. Here we ask:

When you need to reconnect with yourself, what are your best ways? (e.g., walking in nature, gardening, meditating, connecting with a special person)

Or: *Can you remember a time where you really felt a great connection to yourself and the larger world?*

Once a client identifies such a place—and sometimes they first need a little coaching on how to relax, breathe, slow down—then it is experientially "unpacked," so the positive elements of that memory are revivified in the present state.

That's great. So, when you garden, that usually shifts you into a really positive state. Can you remember a time—perhaps recently—where you felt a very positive gardening experience?

Step 3: Mindfulness Drops of Silence (for the Verbal Mind)

Now we tune to the second mind, your verbal mind. Feel where you sense the physical location of your verbal mind... The front of your head?... one side?... a bit outside your body?... isn't that interesting that you can sense its locations? And as you affectionately sense your verbal mind, just notice what's happening with it... is it tense? Tired? Bored?... whatever you notice: *Welcome... welcome... welcome*.

And to nurture it with soul medicine, imagine holding a second seed between your thumb and your index finger. *A seed of silence* ...And slowly lift that seed above your head... 3-4 times slower than an ordinary movement...and then drop it gently into the heart of your verbal mind... letting it open a beautiful nest of golden silence to hold the verbal mind. *Silence... silence... silence*. You're not trying to get rid of your inner voices... just hold them in a beautiful "energy ball" of luminous silence... Feel affection and compassion for how hard your mind works... how worried it gets... how insecure it can feel... bring it inside the golden ball of silence... *Welcome... welcome... welcome...* (Pause)

Step 4: Mindfulness Drops of Spaciousness (for the Field Mind)

And then the third mind is all the relationship communities you live in and are a part of... your workplace... your family... your friends... all the different relationship communities to which you belong... And to bring soul medicine there... take hold of a third seed... *the seed of spaciousness*... Sense that seed, feel it pulsating between your fingers, sense its colors and pulsations... *Spacious... spacious... spacious...*

And slowly lift that seed over the top of your head...let it drop gently through your mind-body... and as it touches your center... the heart... or your belly... let that seed open and bloom a beautiful generative field that ripples out into the world... just like watching the ripples in a pond when a pebble is dropped... A beautiful, luminous field... just unfolds and spreads. *Spacious... spacious... spacious...* to include all the people and places and things in that situation... and opens even beyond that... *your COACH* field expands to include everything... making room for all of it, locking onto none of it...*spacious... spacious... spacious...*Room for you, room for them, room for the unity of all life. (This can be elaborated.)

Step 5: Integration and reorientation

So notice how the seeds can help you remember... *you have a body, but even deeper, you have a body of bodies* to have and to hold your precious body...*You have a verbal mind...but you are the mind of minds* that can affectionately hold every thought with loving kindness...you are in many relationships, but you can feel the deeper presence that permeates and extends beyond each relationship.

So, take a few moments to sense what you've sensed... to notice what you've learned about your own creative power... and anything you find here that's useful... take a vow to keep practicing it every day... knowing that your life is lived by the promises you make...as a child, we mostly make negative vows: *I'll never be like that...I'll never do that...*but as grown-ups, our lives grow from the positive vows we take...

And then when you're ready, give yourself a nice hug. Our teacher Virginia Satir, the great earth mother of family therapy, used to say that to be a human being, you need at least 10 hugs a day. You can always give yourself at least 5 of those... so give yourself a hug... give yourself the love you long to receive... give yourself the message: *I love you, I care for you, I am here for you...* and then when you're ready, take a nice deep breath, open your eyes, and come back into ordinary reality.

This process can be modified in many different ways. In volume 1, we talked about how we usually secure a commitment from each client for daily practices, and then support them in finding which practices are optimal to them. This "mindfulness drops" process is one of the most popular, many people finding great benefit from it. People use it in different ways: Right before a difficult challenge, as a brief COACH connection at spare moments in the day, as part of a daily self-care process, etc. It really helps develop the deeper organic intelligence that is a COACH field. This has its own intrinsic value, but it also allows a person to more freely let go of their ego struggles, as they feel there's something deeper to "catch" them when they surrender.

Opening the COACH field: Mindfulness Mantras

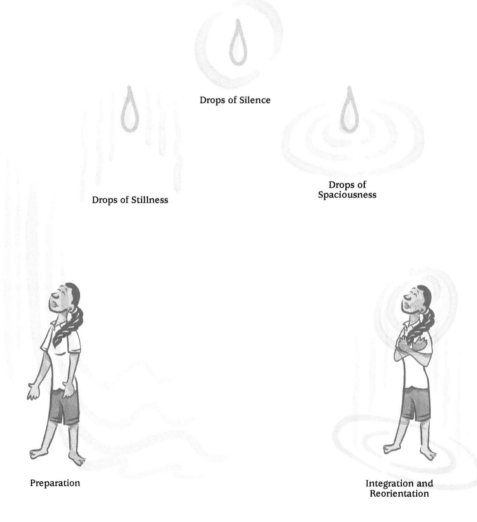

Drops of Silence

Drops of Stillness

Drops of Spaciousness

Preparation

Integration and Reorientation

The Three-point Attention Technique

We have talked about how it's one thing to develop a COACH state, and quite another thing to maintain it. We lose our COACH connection so easily, in so many ways. Things start out so well and then derail so easily. So, it's especially important to have ways to stay centered, especially in areas where we know we're easily triggered. The technique of three-point attention is very effective in this regard.

In aikido, a central principle is,

> *Never give your eyes to the attacker!*

A corollary would be,

> *Never give your mind away to the problem!*

In doing so, we lose our center and CRASH significantly. The three-point attention technique is a way to develop the "soft eyes" that allow the prime aikido connection of: **Drop into center, open into field.** This is a COACH practice of relaxing the body, dropping attention into the hands, feeling the eyes as soft and clear, and making peripheral attention dominant. In this embodied, open awareness, you can enter a *flow state* in which information/energy moves *through* you, minimizing CRASH dangers and optimizing COACH possibilities.

This is not a sentimental or "warm fuzzy" state; it's actually the performance state used in aikido to creatively engage with severe attacks and threats. Let's first touch upon the basic core of the technique, and then consider different applications.

1. **Step 1: Settle in, settle down.** As with most Generative Coaching techniques, you can do this sitting or standing, but we suggest you start with sitting. Get a comfortable posture, straight spine, hands palms down on your legs. Take a few deep breaths and relax.

2. **Step 2: Open the vertical axis** "heaven/earth" connection. Breathe up and down your spine, imagining a vertical axis that breathes down into the earth, then up through the crown of the head into "heaven." Do this in a relaxed way, sensing your mind "riding the breath" between heaven and earth, opening a luminous vertical channel. Very importantly, feel the weight in the lower half of your body, letting your mind drop into your belly center.

3. **Step 3: Develop "soft eyes" and open peripheral awareness.** We usually carry a lot of tension in our eyes, which creates the ego chatter of the mind. To release this *neuromuscular lock*, feel your eyes as "soft", perhaps imagining them as "radiant suns." Not a glazed or drugged look, but clear and "without static". Find a feeling of expansive subtle awareness, opening your peripheral mind as dominant. This is a practice: once you know what you're looking for, explore each time how to find it.

4. **Feel your two hands in your peripheral awareness as the first two points of attention.** This allows you to drop your attention down, connect it to somatic resonance, open it up to a COACH field, and anchor it into the two hands. Like any practice, it may take a while to really settle into this connection; the conditioned ego mind is forever breaking rhythm and connection. You'll know you've found it when you feel a positive, quiet field opening all around you, with you present at its center. (This is a COACH field.)

5. **Find a third point of attention to complete a "triangle."** This could be an imaginary point in front of you, which would open your mind out into the world. Or it could be a center point inside your body—for example, your belly or lower back—which would support you to stay connected with yourself, not losing yourself to other people. Find which is more helpful to you.

6. **Put all the pieces togeth-er.** Now you can practice a "holon" where all these expe-riences harmonize: *Relaxed body... straight spine... ver-tical flow... soft eyes, open peripheral awareness... focus softly on two hands... include a third point.*

This is a basic practice for opening a COACH field. It is a cousin to meditational techniques such as *mantra* repetition or *mindful breathing,* but the gentle focus on the hands and open peripheral attention brings consciousness more fully into the world, allowing for creative action. As I said, it is a core practice in aikido: Soft eyes, relaxed body, open awareness, grounded focus. It helps you to relax and connect, but also to creatively perform. To get a feel for how that might work, let's examine a few applications.

1. Dissolving anxiety. If you were to teach others fail-safe techniques for creating anxiety, anytime and anywhere, what exercises would you give them? What body posture, breathing patterns, internal dialogue, forehead movements... especially, eye tension and movements? I think we would find agreement: To develop anxiety, you have to tense your body, inhibit your breathing, scrunch your forehead, and tense your eyes and look around in a darting, fearful way. Right?

The three-point attention technique is a great pattern interrupter for anxiety. *Relaxed body, somatic center, soft eyes, grounded soft focus of hands, peripheral awareness.* Doing this, it's virtually impossible to become anxious. Clients may need coaching to be willing and able to release the compulsive anxiety patterns, and then daily practices to develop an alternative experience of a COACH field. But we've seen time and time again that this can be done, especially with the three-point method.

2. Dissolving insomnia. Similar to anxiety, how would you teach someone to be an insomniac? How about: Tell yourself you have to go to sleep, toss and turn, barely breathe, get worried about tomorrow, lock your eyes, move around in an arrhythmic way, get upset with yourself for not relaxing... the usual suspects.

We are global travelers, and jet lag can disrupt sleep patterns. So, we've used a modified version of the three-point technique. First, get in bed; lay flat on your back and take a few deep breaths; slowly do a "body scan," using the traditional technique of deliberately tensing a muscle area for the count of 5, then deeply exhaling and releasing/ relaxing.

Next, develop soft eyes, and feel "soft hands", each hand palm up on the bed. Now focus on an imaginary point above you (presumably in the dark), so you tune into the three points—soft (left) hand, soft (right) hand, imaginary point. If you're tense and wound up, it may take gentle coaching to keep bringing your attention back; remember, yelling at yourself is probably the best way to prolong the negative state. Connect with the three-point absorption until you wake up refreshed in the morning.

3. Keeping your center with difficult "others." We've all experienced being overwhelmed by certain types of people: A very critical person; or a client pleading with you to save them; or someone who narcissistically demands continual attention. It's easy to get "hypnotized" by their emotional energy and abandon ourselves. These are examples of what is meant by "giving your center away" to another person.

The three-point attention method is a really practical way to stay connected with yourself as a base for opening safely and skillfully to others. It's a version of a general 4-step process: (1) connect to center; (2) open to field (beyond any person, place, or thing); (3) feel a resonance with the other (person), only in a way that keeps the first two connections; and (4) feel a "giving and receiving" between self and other.

Again, a commitment to keeping the three points allows easy "testing" of a COACH state. As soon as you (or your client) starts to lose the connection, it's easily noticeable, signaling that CRASH is knocking on your door. So, we train this process of connecting to a grounded, open self as the requirement for opening to others.

Doing this can also allow you a much deeper connection. I learned from Milton Erickson to go into something like a three-point attention state in listening to clients. Not only do you not get hypnotized by the story—which is usually being used as a distraction technique in problem areas—but it allows you to feel the person's somatic center and its experience. We will see in Step 5 how this can be done through a process of *relational centering*, which allows "center to center" connections with clients. For now, we simply want to emphasize how you can stay with yourself as the precondition for having any chance to help others.

4. Keeping your center when emotionally triggered. When we're doing challenging work, it can easily trigger unintegrated emotion that can quickly tail-spin into significant CRASH. I used to work a lot with trauma survivors, where this danger is paramount. I learned to usually ask clients to keep their eyes open during such work, to feel more secure grounding.

We often use the three-point attention as a grounding technique to stay in the "here and now." The "third point" would be me; or sometimes, clients would ask that my golden retriever "sit in" on the session, and a hand on his back would provide far safer grounding than I could. The open-eyed three-point attention allows instant detection of the onset of a potential CRASH state, which would signal an immediate movement to re-establishing COACH: *pause... relax... slow down... reconnect to hands... reconnect to me.* This is a process of learning to commit to yourself to only open (to another person, to a difficult experience) in a way and a rate that allows you to remain connected to yourself and the field of resources. This "deep listening" to your organic consciousness is the single most important commitment you can make.

5. Staying in COACH with difficult questions. In a creative life, there are many times when we want to go forward, but don't know how. The three-point method can really help with this challenge of sitting with a question that has no immediate answer. A typical response to such a challenge is a CRASH state. You can see this by asking someone caught in such a struggle for a *somatic model* of it. Lots of tension, frustration, self-punitive gestures, and so forth.

Generative learning always occurs at our "edge," the place between "knowing" and "not knowing." So these "questions with no obvious answers" have really high creative potential, if we can hold them in a COACH field. We sometimes joke that the favorite words of our mentor, Milton Erickson, were, *I don't know!* We would be surprised by how often he would say these words, and how happy he was to hear them from his students or patients. We learned from him that these words heralded a threshold into generative change, if positive conditions were present. In fact, Erickson's full statement was usually: *I don't know... but I'm very curious to find out!* He taught us that the experience of not-knowing is precisely why and when "trance"—and what we call the COACH field— is helpful. It is a way to shift from "searching for the answer" to securely "holding the question," so that a deeper intelligence can step forward and guide the way. (In the 4-step creativity model we touched upon in Chapter 1, this is the *incubation* period.)

Three-point attention is a superb way to work with these questions that have no obvious answer. The base method is: *Settle down... somatic relaxation and vertical flow...soft eyes...three points of attention.* For this application, you can then invite the person to use the three points to imagine a triangle that opens a passage deep into the quantum unconscious. With that attunement, invite them to hold their core question, like a gentle mantra. *Speak the question... turn it over to the deeper presence... open to whatever comes... (repeat).* With the peripheral soft focus grounded in somatic wisdom, become curious about any images, symbols, and new understandings that rise from the "deep well" of the unconscious, up through the triangle, into their field awareness. Obviously, this process is done with the *rhythm, resonance, and repetition* needed for creative work. Hopefully, you can see how it can be a great tool for the "conscious/creative unconscious" conversation crucial to generative creativity.

Summary

Ok. That's a lot. Let's start wrapping up this exploration of this crucial first step of opening a COACH field. We now have touched upon four basic methods for doing this: (1) revivifying COACH-like experiences; (2) guided process of C-O-A-C-H; (3) the three mindfulness drops; and (4) the three-point attention technique. For each step of generative coaching, you need a number of methods in your toolbox. You've now got four for Step 1, many more to come!

In all of this, we learn that COACH and CRASH states are not absolute, fixed forms. Organic consciousness, like everything in nature, is in constant change. We don't think of COACH vs. CRASH as artificial distinctions imposed on organic consciousness, as Western traditions too often do. They are ways of talking about how to weave sensitive human presence into the organic consciousness of life. When we are awake and open, a whole new dimension of creative life becomes present; we benefit from life and life benefits from us. But when we are closed and hostile—what we are calling CRASH—a dark consciousness unique to humans poisons organic consciousness. We hurt the world, and the world is hurt by us.

We knew Milton Erickson in his final five years. He was an old man and to us, he knew everything. We were therefore surprised to hear him say things like, *The more I learn, the more I realize how little I know.* We thought for sure he was lying. Now as we "mature," those words resonate the truth. So, what we're seeking in this first step is how to join human consciousness into the interconnected unity of all life. We know now that we can only do so if we realize that each day, each moment, how to do that "in the weave of the total complex," is unique. *I don't know, but I'm really curious to find out...*

Throw yourself like seed as you walk, and into your own field,
don't turn your face for that would be to turn it to death,
and do not let the past weigh down your motion.

~ Miguel De Unamuno
Roots and Wings
edited and translated by
Robert Bly

Chapter 3

Step 2
Positive Intention

The central question at the core of generative coaching conversations is:

What is it you most want to create in your life?

In the last chapter, we focused on *opening a COACH field* as a first step in that conversation. Now we focus on the complementary step of *setting a positive intention* in a generative way.

To understand "generative" intention, let's return to the "4E" model touched upon in Chapter 1. There we saw how cognitive science has shifted from "disembodied intellect" thinking—where an idea is some verbal concept you hold in your head—to multi-modal models of ideas as: *embodied, embedded (in multiple contexts), expressive (involving nonverbal "music" and movements),* and *enactive (actual behavior patterns).* This makes it clear that if we are coaching creativity, we need to ensure that clients resonantly connect to each of these modalities.

We think it unfortunate that people-helping traditions like coaching and therapy emerged from medical/scientific contexts, where the disembodied intellect is the default value. We think coaching is better done when life is regarded as *performance art*. Because in performance art, we're really working with the question of how to find your deepest connection to life and then touch people with it. That's the question that we're living in generative coaching.

In *GC1*, we suggested that a prototype model of doing that involved deep connection with three representational modalities:

1. *Verbal:* as a declaration or injunction: *Let's make THIS happen!*

2. *Visual* (envision a positive future)

3. *Somatic* (embody it)

We saw how we find it best for the verbal statement to be *succinct* (five words or less), *positive* (the presence of a specific behavior, achievement, or experiential state), and *resonant* (in both client and coach). For example:

I want a deeper intimacy in my marriage.

The visual (preferably color) image might be either a social reality or a metaphor. For example:

And a color image that goes with that is... my partner and I hugging (social reality)

OR

Two birds flying together in the sky (metaphorical image)

It's usually best to have a combination of reality-based and metaphorical images.

The somatic representation is usually a **somatic model**:

And if I ask my body to show that as a movement, it might be... (a movement of one hand opening out, the other touching the heart)

Clients are usually asked to slowly move through this 3-part statement (with **rhythm, resonance,** and **repetition**), like a song or dance. For example, a client struggling with his work partners spoke the following:

What I most want to create in my professional relationship is... mutual respect and deep listening.

And a visual image that might go with that is... (client is coached to slow down, see what comes)... *sitting with my partners and listening...*

Somatic model of first round

Somatic model of second round

Somatic model of third round

And if I ask my somatic mind to let a somatic model come, it might be... (pause)... (client touches heart and slowly nods head)...

A second round produced the three content statements of *open-heartedness (verbal), a man meditating in the forest (visual),* and *closed eyes/two hands on heart (somatic model).* A third round: *deep understanding (verbal) / walking on the beach with partners (visual)/ salsa dancing (somatic model).* For each statement and each round, the creative process is deepened with: *resonance, pausing, silence, feedback, breathing, repeating.* In other words, the words are just one part of the creative conversation, as in any performance art.

As if often the case, the client shared that as he did the process, it felt like he was "shedding skins" and "dissolving walls" that he had built up, allowing a much deeper, clearer sense of who he wanted to be, and how he wanted to communicate in this relationship. He reported later how much of a difference it made when he went back to work.

Life is a performance art. When we get caught up in our heads, lost in our emotions, disconnected from others, it doesn't matter what we want: nothing positive can happen. Connecting clients to their positive intention involves safely and skillfully connecting them to the deepest parts of their selves. From there, dreams can be realized.

Speaking Intention

1. What I most want to create in my life is (*verbal statement*).

2. The *image* that goes with that is _____.

3. And the *somatic model* of that is (show movement).

First Method:
Extending Intention to Touch Others – "Energy Balls"

Connecting deeply with one's self is good, but not enough. We also need to deeply bring ourselves into the world and touch others with who we are and what we're up to. Some of our best teachers are children: there's no boundary (for better and worse) between them and the world. Their spontaneity and energy are amazing, they touch so deeply. We were all children like that once… What happened? We learned along the way to put up invisible "energy walls." It makes sense: We had to learn to protect ourselves from negative energy, and we were taught to suppress our spontaneous "peacock" energy. When you look at the embodied presence of young children vs. grown adults, you see the difference: *Adults live behind invisible energy walls.*

Most adults live behind invisible energy walls. Nothing gets out or in.

The cost is enormous: nothing gets out, nothing gets in. We suffer what Henry David Thoreau called "lives of quiet desperation." To be creative, you have to open your channels and touch the world with your spirit, like a singer singing her song, or an orator's presence reaching out across a room.

To be creative you have to open your channels and touch the world with your spirit.

One way we coach clients to do that is an exercise called "throwing energy balls." In this process, the coach stands across from the client. The client is helped to connect with a positive intention, imagine it as an "energy ball" that they are holding, then practice "throwing the ball" to touch people with that intention. This magnifies the experience of touching others with an unbroken fluid movement: Feel the intention, put in an energy ball, make connection to the coach, throw the energy ball while speaking the intention, "splash" the coach with it, release, come back to center. It's easy to see in doing so where the person hits "CRASH" and how to embody and extend COACH versions of intention in many different ways.

1. Coach and client face each other: COACH state, identify goal, place in "energy ball."

2. Client throws "energy ball intention" towards Coach (or imaginary others): *What I most want to bring into the world is... X!*

3. After initial exchange, coach and client improvise multiple ways to touch others with intention.

4. Return to center, review, notice what needs further work, commitment, reorient.

Let's take a look at session excerpts with a client named Olivia.

Step 1: Social Connection, Informal Goal Setting

As in any social connection, we usually start with a bit of casual conversation to make connection, and then ask the client to informally talk about what they most want to achieve in the session.

Steve: *Hi, Olivia.*

Olivia: *Hi, Steve.*

Steve: *Welcome to the session. How's it going today?*

Olivia: *Pretty good. I'm enjoying the sunny day!*

Steve: *Me too. It feels like spring is finally arriving.*

Olivia: *Yeah.*

(A few more minutes of small talk ensue.)

Steve: *So, let's talk a little bit about the work you want to do today. Can you tell me, if there's one thing that you'd love to leave here today having accomplished, what would that be?*

Olivia: *I have an old behavior. I start to worry about talking to someone, and then I get kind of wound up and speak really fast to the person... I would like to change this part of my communication. I think it would improve my professional and personal skills.*

Steve: *Yeah. I can hear and see and feel that you're touching something meaningful for you. And I would really like to support you in doing that.*

Olivia: *Thank you.*

Steve: *If there was one area where this is especially important... where would that be? Something in your professional life? Your personal life?*

(**Note:** It's usually important to connect the intention to a specific context, that's where the creative imagination activates, and the core dynamics of the situation are revealed.)

Olivia: *It would be in my personal relationship with my husband...* (pauses, looks tearful).

Steve: *(touches hands on his chest): Yeah, when you mention that, I feel it touch my heart in a deep way. I don't know where you feel it most deeply?*

Olivia: (Touches her chest): *Somewhere here...*

Steve: (Silently breathes a few moments, touching heart.) *Yeah, I feel that. Great. I would like to just welcome that presence into our conversation. Welcome!* (Olivia nods, hand touching her heart.) *And if I'm understanding correctly, you're saying that you love your husband very much and would like to support him...* (Steve extends arms out)... *but when you go to do it, something chaotic starts to happen...* (Steve makes chaotic, anxious movements)... *and you get overwhelmed. Did I understand that correctly?*

Olivia: *Right, Stephen. Yeah, that's exactly right.*

(As is often the case, when the client connects to her goal, it activates an obstacle: *I want X, but Y shows up.* This is a good time to open a COACH state so the obstacle can be welcomed and transformed into as an essential resource.)

Step 2: Develop a COACH State

Steve: *Well, to make room for the whole team— your goal, your obstacle, and whomever else might drop by in the conversation—it's probably a good time to open a positive COACH space.*

Olivia: *That sounds like a good idea.*

Steve: *Do you have a good way that works for you, to connect to a positive state?*

Olivia: *Yes. It's usually a breathing process. I slowly breathe in* (brings hands above her head) *and then breathe out, and let everything go (brings hands down slowly, breathes out).*

Steve: (mirrors the hand movement)*: Great. And if it's ok with you, let's just take a few minutes and you can walk me through that process. I'll stay in my own lane over here, but let's see how we might each use that process to develop a positive state... Can you walk us through it?*

Olivia: (Nods) *Breathe in...* (slowly repeating the hand movement) *and lift your arms up* (arms life slowly)*... then let them down... and let go and breathe out as you do.* (Deep exhale as arms come down.)

(This is repeated a few times, to the benefit of all.)

Steve: *Great. Thanks. And are there any visual images that go with that... places in nature? Other positive images?*

Olivia: (Breathing deeply, eyes closed). *It's like I'm going down to the water, like under the water, but it's really nice. The water is really warm and I can relax and totally surrender. I can be supported.*

Steve: *Awesome. So, let's use that as our (COACH) base. Breathing, slowing down... feeling the body move... feeling the warm waters that support you... you can just sink down...* (This is elaborated for a bit.)

And that's always our first step. We owe it to ourselves, before stepping into a challenge, to take the time and reconnect to resources. To feel: I'm safe... I'm OK... Feel the water... Feel the beauty of the sea... And whenever you feel yourself getting caught up in any of the old stuff – the worry, the agitation, the talking faster – this is probably the single most important thing you can do for yourself. Use stress as a red flag... a signal... when to get back... to the sea, body, to the breath.

It looks you have a nice positive connection, now, am I right?

Olivia: *Yes, very much.*

Steve: *Great. So, stay connected with that place... with your rhythm, your breathing, your body, your mind... And with that connection, open your eyes and let's see how we can use it a resource.*

Olivia: *Great. Thank you.*

Step 3: Generative Statement of Intention

Steve: *You're welcome. So. let's return to your goal and see how to deepen the connection with it. Staying connected to your COACH state, let yourself speak the intention in five words of less, with a somatic movement.*

Olivia: *What I most want to do is... to support my husband.* (Her voice gets constrained, her shoulders lock.)

Steve: (Gently) *I can see and feel that you really want to support your husband... and as you go* *to do that, something else in you shows up. Your shoulders lock, you look stressed. That's interesting... I'm sure that makes sense. To that part of you, I say... welcome!*

Olivia: (laughing)*: I just feel something immediately here* (she tightens shoulder and arms) *that's really angry.*

Steve: *Yeah. I had this image of a 7-year-old girl, very intense, very isolated– I don't know what images you might find connected to that emotion...*

Olivia: (touches throat and upper chest area). *Well... when I was around that age, my mother, who was a doctor, was always very very busy. She looked so overwhelmed and unhappy. And I wanted so badly to support her.* (**Note:** This is the intention for Olivia in her present family.)

But I didn't know what to do. She seemed to just ignore me, and I would get confused and just speak really fast. And then she would get angry at me and walk out of the room.

Steve: *You mean like...* (Steve tenses, speaks faster). *"I want to support them, but they're not receiving it. I better try harder, speak faster."* (Steve speeds up, playfully starting to babble.)

Olivia: *Yeah. Exactly. Exactly. That's exactly it.*

Steve: (Calms, speaks gently.) *I see that. I feel that. I welcome and offer support for that 8-year-old presence that comes up when you want to support your husband.*

(Olivia tears up, and Steve gently helps her reconnect to the "warm supportive waters" of her COACH state.)

And isn't it great that as you go to bring more support into your family, something inside of you wakes up and says, Hey, me too!?

Olivia: (nods her head, still touching chest gently)

(**Note:** Again, obstacles often activate when a positive intention is spoken. In *GC*, we see them as resources that are integral parts of the generative solution.)

Steve: *If I'm understanding correctly, it's really important for you to offer support to your husband.* (Makes movement outward)... *But you're learning that to do that, you have to receive support for yourself first.*

Olivia: (quiet for a few moments, then nods, looks relieved)

Steve: *Good to know... So why don't we try this modified statement: I really want to support you... but I also need your support.*

Olivia: (Pauses, then nods head. Speaks the two-part statement slowly, several times.) *Yes, that feels so different. So right... Something calms down inside. Something slows down. That really fits.*

Steve: *Great, good to know.*

Step 4: Extending and receiving intention with somatic models

Steve: *So, let's see how you can get that message into play with your husband.*

Olivia: *Ok.*

Steve: (standing across from Olivia). *I'd like to gently coach you through a simple sequence.* (Each of the following statements is spoken with **rhythm, resonance, repetition**.) *COACH state...* (Olivia breathes and opens her arms.) *Connect to intention: I want to support you... and I need you to support.* (One hand touches her heart, the other extends out.) *COACH state to hold that intention...*

Now let's find a somatic movement that goes with each side. As you say, I want to support you, let yourself imagine holding that intention as an energy ball... (Steve models) *and then when you speak those worlds... I want to support you... throw an energy ball to me.* (Steve models) *I'll be the social representative of your husband...throw an energy ball to me... splashing him... touching him... I want to SUPPORT you...* (throws ball to Olivia like an innocent child with carefree abandonment.)

Ok, you try...

(Olivia is now coached to throw the energy ball of her intention like a playful child, no holding back. As with most clients, this takes a few minutes of coaching, especially around moving with the somatic child-like energy of a child at play. Olivia does it a few times, but then starts to CRASH.)

Steve: *Great. Let's pause. Listen to your body, listen to what inner truth is telling you... Isn't it good to notice, that as you go to bring support to others, something inside of you shows up and says, What about me? Did someone say support? I could use a little support!* (This is done gently, the intent being to invite the part that usually shuts the system down to be welcomed as an integral resource and contributor.)

So, let's use your body's feedback to shift to the other side. This deep inner need speaking: And I need you to support me. Make a movement of that. Send the message (as a somatic model), and show the need (somatic model of receiving back.) Offer support... demand support. I give it to you... I need it from you. (As Olivia moves through these somatic movements of throwing and receiving energy balls, some deep shift begins to happen. A beautiful child/woman beauty emerges, it feels like it fills the room.)

Steve: *That's it. There it is. There you are... Feel that wholeness... of giving and receiving... That's it. Feel what it's like to find that balance. You can only authentically give to others if you're receiving back in a balanced way.*

Olivia: *Wow, that's such a deep shift. Things feel open. Everything. When I'm right now thinking about those contexts, they don't elicit that self-blaming anymore. I can feel how that tension and anxiety... and the deep exhaustion that I feel all day... is released when I ask to be supported.*

Steve: *That's it. That's it. Good for you. That's it.*

This is continued for another 8-10 minutes, with Olivia sensing all the different parts of her that need to be honored and integrated for her to bring support to others in an authentic way.

To succeed with our positive intention, we need to congruently embody it, then extend and release into the world. On this path, we come up against the many obstacles that hold us back, and in GC we see them as precisely holding the resources we need for creative wholeness. Exercises like "throwing energy balls" is a fun, illuminating way that we can coach people into extending themselves in a unbroken circle of connection with the world.

Extending Intention to Touch Others – "Energy Balls"

STEP 1:
CONNECT TO
INTENTION

STEP 2:
GENERATE A
COACH STATE

> I REALLY WANT TO SUPPORT YOU... BUT I ALSO NEED YOUR SUPPORT

ACKNOWLEDGE OBSTACLES WHENEVER THEY APPEAR

STEP 3: GENERATIVE STATEMENT OF INTENTION

STEP 4: EXTEND AND RECEIVE YOUR INTENTION USING SOMATIC MODELS (ENERGY BALL)

Second Method: Extending Intention with Tenderness, Fierceness, and Playfulnes

There is a second part to this that we want to touch upon here. (We'll explore it further in the next chapter.) It is what we call *the three archetypal energies* of tenderness, fierceness, and playfulness. An archetype is a universal human pattern evolved over many generations in dealing with core human challenges.

Sometimes we most need to be gentle, peaceful, and kind-hearted; this is the archetypal pattern of *tenderness. Who is an example to you of somebody with deep powerful tenderness?*

The complement is *fierceness*: we also need to be tough, committed, resilient, have good boundaries, be a good bullshit-detector. *Who is a model for you of positive fierceness?*

We also need *playfulness*. Life is much too serious to not have a good sense of humor. We need to bring sparkle and an "Irish twinkle" into connections. *Who is a representative of playfulness for you?*

Think of any creative or inspirational person, and you will find they carry all three of these energies in integrated ways. We will explore this more in the next chapter. For now, let's just look at how adding archetypal energies can deepen the extension of intention into the world.

Who could be your role models for tenderness, fierceness and playfulness?

1. Continue improvisations of "throwing energy balls" to touch others with generative intention.

2. Include somatic models/energies of positive fierceness, playfulness, and tenderness.

3. Sense optimal connections, make note and vows.

Steve: *So, Olivia, I'd like to add another piece to this work, which is the energy you're embodying when you put your intention into action. Sometimes we need most of all to bring* **tenderness**, *first to ourselves, and then from there, maybe others. At other times, we really need* **positive fierceness**: *we need to let people know we're serious, we're taking a stand, that we bring our positive fire to the connection. And then at others, we need to be able to play, to not be so grim and uptight… to be able to twinkle and sparkle.*

I'd like to ask you to consider this relational connection with your husband, and what you're trying to create… and I'm wondering, which of those energies—tenderness, fierceness, playfulness—do you think is your weak link?

Olivia: *Fierceness. I think I'm afraid of it. It consumed by mother, and so I try to stay away from it.*

Steve: *That makes sense. So, when you think of fierceness, you've especially got this CRASH version of your mom's anger…*

Olivia: *Yes…*

Steve: *And do you remember making a promise that you'd never be like your mom?* (twinkles).

Olivia: *Yes, I did.*

Steve: (Laughs, nodding.) *It's not so much that I'm psychic, but I've discovered that almost every one of us makes promises that we'll never be like our parent. I certainly did.* (Steve and Olivia laugh.)

Steve: *Well, you know, the negative vows we make in the first half of our life, we usually have to break in the second half. It sounds like you need to break your promise to stay away from fierceness.* (pause) *Without it, you can't ever ask for what you need. And if you can't love yourself, it's impossible to bring authentic love to others…*

Olivia: (nods head). *Yeah, I think you're right.*

Steve: *What I want to emphasize is that there are negative and positive versions of each of these energies. It sounds like you suffered the negative versions of fierceness growing up in your family... I did, too. But now we have to learn the positive versions, so we can be integrated and whole. I wonder... if you take a breath and close your eyes for a moment... and just let an image come of a positive fierceness... just notice what appears.*

Olivia: (Laughs) *So strange... but I got this image of a Japanese sumo wrestler* (laughs). *I don't know why, it's not something I'm usually interested in, but that's what showed up.*

Steve: *Isn't that interesting? So, let's welcome this sumo wrestler. I'm sure he's arrived to support your process.* (Both laugh.). *Let's try this experiment, shall we?* (Steve begins to model and Olivia follows.) *Let's get into the somatic model of a sumo wrestler.* (Each foot stomping the ground, squatting down, hands on knees, making sounds, looking fierce but playful.)

Olivia: *Oh my god...* (laughs hysterically).

Steve: *Come on, join me.* (Steve and Olivia begin to somatically model the sumo wrestler, both laughing while also fierce). *And let's try this: One foot stomps... the other foot stomps... I need your support!* (With fierce, vulnerable expression.). *I need your support! Damn it, I need your support.*

Olivia: (Olivia starts exploring it, moving through looks of anger, vulnerability, laughter.) *I need your support.* (Adds a few more statements)

Steve: *And now let's shift.* (Extends arm and palm out) *And I want to support you.* (Comes up to a gentle posture, eyes tender but clear.)

Now you try it on your own...

Olivia: (Slowly drops into sumo posture... looks to the side... repeats the movement more slowly with bouncing in the knees, extends one hand, looks serious): *I'm here to support.* (Brings out the other hand.) *And I need your support, too.*

(It is really good when the client starts improvising their own movements. They are finding their own connection to their creative power.)

Steve: *Good.*

Olivia: *Is it fierce enough?* (Bows like a Japanese swordsman, smiles, laughs.)

Steve: *I felt it. You really got my attention. I was listening, like, "Wow, okay!"*

Olivia: *It's interesting Stephen, because I thought in those situations, I'm pretty fierce. But now, what I am aware, no, it's not fierce. It's weakness, it's just expressing like with that* (waves arms, makes decisive hand movement).

Steve: *I hear you. T.S. Eliot called it "the impotence of rage."*

Olivia: *Probably people think it's fierce, but it's different emotionally.*

Steve: *It's the difference between what we would call a CRASH version of fierceness, which is just destructively blaming people, but it's pretty helpless... to positive fierceness, which is: "See me. Care for me. Give me support." That's what we call the COACH version.* (Olivia nods and breathes deeply.)

Awesome. Ok if we stop here? You did a wonderful job.

Olivia: *Yeah, it's a good place to stop. Thanks so much.*

Project your positive intention by
throwing an energy ball

Add tenderness, fierceness or
playfulness with a somatic model

Summary

It don't mean a thing, if it ain't got that swing,
—Duke Ellington

Here I am in my middle way, having wholly lost my way.
—Dante

Between the desire and the spasm, falls the Shadow.
—T.S. Eliot

**Let your creative spirit touch the world with
your positive intention.**

Our clients do not lack intelligence, motivation or resources. They come to us because in the course of living, they have become ensnared in the *samsara* of disconnection. Our job is to help them reconnect to what Bateson called "the weave of the total complex." Contemporary cognitive science understands thinking as not only verbal thought in the head, but ideas that are *embodied, embedded, expressive,* and *enactive*. We have seen in this chapter how generative intention must positively connect to each of these. May the ego return to the interconnectedness of all life.

Last night as I was sleeping,
I dreamt—marvelous error!—
that a spring was breaking
out in my heart.
I said: Along which secret aqueduct,
Oh water, are you coming to me,
water of a new life
that I have never drunk?

—Antonio Machado

Chapter 4

Step 3 – Establish a Generative State

Translating our dreams into reality is a tough challenge, so we need to know how to develop a sustainable COACH state. This "high performance" state has general qualities that are organized differently across contexts. Your best state for negotiating a business contract is hopefully different from your state for enjoying a romantic evening with your sweetheart. Your state for being with young children is hopefully different than when doing martial arts. (This is why traditionally, for example, warriors who had been in battle had to go through a long ritual process before reentering the community.)

IN GC1, we explored the *three positive connections* as the prototype method for developing this generative performance state.

1. Somatic center

2. Positive intention

3. Resources

We want to add two additional methods here. The first is the *archetypal energies—tenderness, fierceness,* and *playfulness—*that we started to explore in the last chapter. The second is what we call the *community of resources*, where you identify and make use of the support team needed to best support your creative journey. We deeply agree with the "inner critic" who tells you,

You're not enough.

But then we add:

Because you're only as good as your support team.

Technique 1: The Three Archetypal Energies: Tenderness, Fierceness, and Playfulness

We saw in the last chapter how the quantum field of the creative unconscious contains the collective narrative of human history (and beyond). From countless experiences of responding to the universal challenges of life, *archetypal deep structures* constellate, activating in a person when new creative responses are called for. *They are core resources needed for creative development.* Each archetype contains 10,000 possible faces; the actual form and value that it assumes depends on the human relationship with them. Archetypal patterns moving through COACH filters become positive resources; when they get trapped in CRASH states, they appear as negative forms.

Here we will focus on how to use somatic models of positive forms of tenderness, fierceness, and playfulness. In Step 5, we will concentrate on "negative" emotions as CRASH versions of an archetypal resource than can be transformed into essential positive resources.

To get a feel for how to use positive archetypal energies, we explore now a 4-step session with a Latin American client named Dan. He is a beautiful man who does personal and professional development programs, and also an exceptional musician and poet.

Step 1: Open COACH Field

Dan and I are both standing. We connect, exchange pleasantries, then I suggest we start by opening a positive space. I make a few general suggestions, then ask him if there's anything he would like to add. He has experience with developing a COACH field, so he walks us both through several minutes of breathing/somatic movements. As he brings his hands to touch his belly center, I take that as a cue to move to the next step.

Step 2: Set Positive Intention

I coach him to stay connected to his center, and ask him to set a positive intention/goal for the session. It takes about 5 minutes of conversation for him to express what in step 2 we identified as a "well-formed" intention:

I want to create a year-long certification program for coaches.

As he speaks this, I comment on the tension that I see develop in his shoulders. He laughs and says it's hard for him to boldly speak his dreams. I commiserate gently and, because the CRASH does seem fairly severe, I suggest that maybe we just do a little dance and song of reconnection. We do this playfully, and it seems to release the CRASH.

I then share an image I had of him welcoming a shy little boy onto his shoulders, and inviting him to "come along for the ride." He is very touched by this, and it seems like a good way to reframe the tension (as a child needing inclusion).

When I ask him how important the goal is, he says, *Very important… 9.5.* Now we're ready to focus on developing the COACH state that will best allow him to succeed on his creative path.

Step 3: Develop generative state (with somatic models of tenderness, positive fierceness, and playfulness.)

In this step we are tuning to each archetypal energy: Tenderness, positive fierceness, and playfulness. The client is invited to develop three different somatic models for each energy. Having only a single map of anything is a recipe for rigidity, so we want clients to feel and creatively move through many maps. This movement keeps them in a creative openness, and allows them to learn which model is most helpful in a given moment.

A. Somatic Models of *Tenderness*

With Dan, I asked which of the three energies he thought would be most helpful to begin with.

Dan: *Well, when you talked about tenderness earlier, something deeply resonated inside of me – being tender with myself, because I am super tender with others, but I'm not sure I'm tender enough with myself.*

I invited him to relax and allow his body to begin moving to find a first somatic model of tenderness. He arrived at a somatic model of his upper body and arms moving slowly.

(In this process, we're finding somatic models by asking the clients to relax and let their body create them. Another way is to have the client identity a representative of that archetypal energy, then "step into" the somatic model of that individual. In both methods the person is coached to relax and let the responses come from within, no force or conscious effort. This "just letting it happen" is crucial for activating creative consciousness.)

I then playfully modeled a young child

saying, *That was great. Let's try it again,* inviting him to find a second somatic model of tenderness. Dan arrived at a somatic model of cradling a baby. I mirrored the movement, and began to hum and sing a lullaby. This seemed to deepen the process, as Dan modeled caressing the baby's head.

I asked him to return to his intention of creating the new training program, to sense any CRASH responses, and respond by "cradling the CRASH," gently saying, *Come to papa.* Dan shared how that illuminated for him that, with tenderness, the first recipient always needed to be himself, and how he sensed the young infant "Dan" as part of his creative process.

I ask him to return to center, make note of that somatic model and its teachings, then find a third somatic model of tenderness. He seemed a bit up in his head, so I encouraged him to just drop a bit deeper, and let his somatic wisdom surprise him. His exploratory movements started to settle into a sort of slow "Hawaiian hula" dance, which we processed a bit:

Dan: *It was interesting – first, when this movement (pushing and bringing in) came, it was like I was rocking a wooden cradle, but then I became the sea, and I was just waves reaching the sand and then going back into the ocean.*

Steve: *Yeah. Awesome.*

Dan: *Just caressing the sand with my hands* (extends hands, palms down).

Steve: *Yeah, I had the feeling from over here that that one helped bring you more out into connection with others – I don't know if that's true.*

Dan: (Nods): *Yes.* (repeats the movement) *Yes. I loved this one, especially being the ocean, caressing the sand.*

Steve: *Yeah. Reminds me of the Hawaiian hula dances* (smiles, both grin and try to do a Hawaiian style dance, laugh). *So, notice: Those are three of ten thousand possibilities. When you say: "Okay, I need to bring tenderness," you don't know exactly what that's going to look like.* (Dan nods.) *But by exploring you can soon discover that may be it's something like this* (pushing and bringing in)... *or maybe something like this* (cradles)... *or maybe like the Hawaiian hula that caresses the sand.* (Both move through the caressing movement, gently and playfully.)

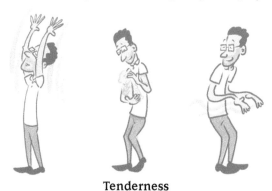

Tenderness

This is an example of how a somatic model might be developed. It's best if it comes spontaneously from within the somatic consciousness. So you're coaching the client into the ***rhythm, resonance,*** and ***repetition*** needed to allow new answers to come from within. It's also good to have multiple models, so the person is learning not to use a fixed posture but to discover the best model for a given situation. The capacity to allow your performance state to shift fluidly, in feedback with the unique patterns of the present moment, is the mark of a champion.

B. Somatic Models of *Positive Fierceness*

A similar process is then used to develop somatic models of the remaining two archetypal energies. Because Dan felt a bit distant from his own positive fierceness, I suggested that he start by identifying an example of positive fierceness out in the world, and then step into that representative. He reported that two images: one of Gandhi (with right hand extending out, fierce but centered), the other of a huge waterfall in Brazil (he raises his hands above his head, and makes the movement of a waterfall).

Steve: *Wow, I feel both of those. So let yourself center and appreciate: To really bring this dream into the world, I need to connect to positive fierceness. Let yourself find your COACH state... set the intention... and step into a somatic model of positive fierceness. It could be the waterfall, it could be Gandhi, it could be...*

Dan: (Starts moving with the somatic model of a waterfall). *It comes with a sound, too.*

Steve: *Yeah, yeah. Great.* (Dan repeats the movement.) *Make sure the sound is in your belly.* (Dan repeats the movement.) *Drop your hips, Dan. Release the shoulders. Be the waterfall. Drop your hips.* (repeats a few times) *Let the fire, the fierceness come lower.* (Dan moves from his hips, his arms extending from his hips. Something shifts, a deeper, earthier energy appears.)

That's it! That's it! Whatever you're touching there, that's it.

Dan: (Extends his arms over his head) *It's interesting – as I drop my hips, the world becomes fire. A wonderful fire. Fire! It's like a volcano.*

Note that as Dan drops his center lower, a third somatic model of positive fierceness as a volcano spontaneously arises. There's a saying in traditional cultures: *a boy becomes a man, and girl becomes a woman, when their hips drop.* Most of us moderns live "upstairs in our heads" with neuromuscular lock, disconnected from the deeper archetypal energies that live "downstairs." In coaching a person to drop their center and hips, often you will see and feel this powerful shift into a mature adult (and ancestral) presence.

So now Dan has three somatic models of positive fierceness: Gandhi, the waterfall, and the volcano. *Multiple maps are needed for a generative state.* In this session, we explored the "fire in the belly" as a positive resource on his journey. He talked about his abusive and violent family, where he learned only very "uncentered forms" of fierceness. At the end of the session, he talked about how one of his most important learnings was that he needed to develop positive fierceness.

Positive Fierceness

C. Somatic Models of Playfulness

Of course, fierceness is not enough. We also need playfulness. We need to enjoy life, put people at ease, not to fall into stultifying seriousness. Interestingly, one of the main casualties of trauma is playfulness. We need to connect with it to be generative.

Dan is a pretty playful guy, so I imagined the interesting challenge would be integrating that playfulness into his fierceness. We came back to COACH, then explored playfulness:

Steve: *And then we have, of course, our third, universal energy of playfulness (opens hands, eyes sparkle, body subtly dances) – which you're pretty good at.* (Dan laughs, nods, and smiles.) *So, let's ask the creative spirits to help us find the many somatic models of playfulness...* (Steve and Dan begin to find a salsa-like dance movement. with movements and sounds.). *Ok, brother Dan, show me a somatic model of playfulness...*

Dan: (Begins to move his hips sideways, he breaks out in a fast Argentinian tango-like dance…)

Steve: *There you go, brother… Olé! Olé! Olé! And as you become that playful dance…feel what it is you're wanting to bring into the world. The teacher you want to become… the programs you want to develop… and let somatic models of playfulness join that process as great, great resources. Olé! Olé! Olé!*

And let's bring the energy down just a bit… finding center… and now let's find additional somatic models for playfulness. Feeling the rhythm… the beat… Let yourself begin a process of declaring your dream, and then adding a somatic movement of playfulness… (Steve models the process:) *I want to create this certification program…* (speaks and moves like a young "peacock")… *and one model of playfulness that I can bring is this* (makes big somatic movement)…

The musical beat and dance movements continue in the connection, while Dan shows one movement (child-like action of jumping up and down), then another (stepping forward playfully to tickle Steve), and then a third (howling like a wolf). He looks and feels great.

Playfulness

Step 4: Make Creative Use of the Archetypal Resources

Once positive somatic models are created, the question becomes how to use them productively.

Steve: *Yeah. And so now, let's just come back to center.* (Steve and Dan do this simultaneously.) *As a first step, come back to that quiet, still point... an open presence... clear... quiet awareness... find your COACH state, deeper than performance... deeper than anything...*

And then add the second step: I'm here... and from here, I connect each day to my intention... feeling the commitment to each day live the path of this intention... and find somatic models for that.

And now the third step of connecting to resources. Find the connections to tenderness, fierceness and playfulness. Start with tenderness... always starting with tenderness to yourself... moving through multiple somatic models of tenderness to find the best ones for your present challenge. (Dan starts with the ocean movement, then to hugging himself, then the "cradling the baby boy".)

And now include positive fierceness. Find and feel those somatic models: Gandhi... the waterfall... the volcanic fire. (Dan moves into "volcanic fire" model.)... *Living the truth: I am not just a nice, sweet boy... Take me seriously...* (Dan continues repeating fire movement.) *Let the fierceness become part of your deepest self.* (As this is elaborated, Dan moves into a warrior stance, both hands/arms extended out fiercely into the world.) *All the bullies... all the people who violated you... all the people who disrespect and try to use you... meet them with your positive warrior stance. No más, amigo. No more... Respect me... respect me... respect me.*

And now to playfulness. Sometimes, those challenges are soooo serious, so easy to get constipated. Remembering the great Irish toast: Don't let the bastards get you down. Instead, finding those deep connections to fierce, tender playfulness... (Dan begins a tango-like movement.) *Imagining the obstacles, dancing like a free warrior spirit...* (Dan's dance becomes like a tai-chi martial art.) *That's it... moving... dancing... playing... Never locking, never freezing, never giving your body and your dance away...* (Dan is improvising now, many movements of fierce, open-hearted play.) *Any time you feel the situation is too tense... too constipated...* (Both laugh.) *Listen to the music, and play... Play with tenderness... play with fierceness... Play seriously with passion and truth and soul... play.* (Steve is silent as Dan continues to improvise his creative dance.)

And then when you're ready, let's come back to center... (breathing, somatic movements back to COACH)...(Steve now speaks very gently.) *And let yourself dance that beautiful process... COACH... positive intention... ancestor energies... moving into action. Let yourself feel that rhythm, that sequence, that deep creative dance. Make a vow to practice each day, know that the principle of impermanence means we have to create it anew each day, in many ways. So, sense what you've done, what your commitments are, what your learnings are for how to realize your dreams. And then when you're ready, take a deep breath and come back into the room.*

In the ensuing discussion, Dan noted that his struggle with fierceness shifted dramatically when he dropped his center and found "the fire." (Again, we say that as long as you live in your head, you'll be afraid and disconnected from your positive soul fire.) He was surprised that playfulness was perhaps the most important addition, easing a "constipated CRASH" state. (Remember, the necessary resource of play is put to sleep by trauma.) Being so rigidly serious, he saw, was a big obstacle.

As I do with all clients, we talked about how this was just a beginning, and that any sustainable changes would require significant post-session work. In generative coaching, this conversation opens the door to the sixth step of committing to practices and homework.

We hope all this gives a sense of how crucial these universal resources of tenderness, positive fierceness, and playfulness are to a positive life. The more creative a life we want to have, the greater the obstacles we will encounter, and the more resilient a performance state we will need. The archetypal energies are crucial elements of a creative response, so it's good to use them as a sort of a quick checklist of what might be needed in a given moment. In other words, we use self-rating levels of each energy—how much tenderness, fierceness, playfulness—to find where we're "low."

A lack of an archetypal energy could just be a limited learning—for example, *When I talk professionally, I can only be serious.* Often, it's a function of stress—as Dan shared, he was so stressed, he forgot his *playfulness.* Or as we'll see in Step 5, a person may only have CRASH versions of an archetypal energy. For example, they may know tenderness only as weakness, co-dependency, or sickening sentimentality; or *fierceness* as rage, relentless criticism, or boundary invasions; or *playfulness* as cynicism, anxious silliness, or not being able to take anything seriously. Because archetypal energies have equal capacity to be positive or negative, depending on how they're humanly held, we may encounter severely negative forms of, say, *fierceness*, and then make a vow to stay as far away from it as possible. This dissociates you from both your self and the very resources needed for a creative life. That's why many people describe learning how to positively connect with each of these energies as one of the most helpful parts of their generative coaching experience.

Using the archetypal energies to establish a generative state

Technique 2: Community of Resources

As the Beatles sang: *We get by with a little help from our friends.* None of us can face a creative challenge in isolation—We will fail when disconnected from our larger community. So, to coach creativity, it's crucial to connect clients with the many positive resources that offer them kinship, blessing and support. The Buddhists call this your *sangha*[1]. Carl Jung called this your *community of saints*—in a mythological, not religious, sense. We call it your *community of resources. A "re-source" is whatever helps you to reconnect to your creative source.* This could be people, places, things; they could be people still living or not, historical figures, ancestors, mythological or spiritual beings. They might be places in nature, or symbolic objects, or art.

We need all sorts of experiential connections to walk a creative path. We need security, encouragement, playfulness, confidence, courage, positive models, guides, just to name a few. Resources are the presences in the world that connect us to these crucial experiences.

In my professional office, you can easily tell who's in my community of resources. You'll see large wall hangings of Milton Erickson, Carl Jung, Morehei Ueshiba (the aikido founder), the medicine (healing) Buddha, and my late great "guru of gurus," Lucky (our family golden retriever). The office is on my home grounds, and it's a sort of refuge for me, a place to regroup and find my way through some challenge. I remember many occasions laying on the couch, opening to long conversations with these extraordinary beings. I can't remember one occasion when it wasn't really helpful.

We think each person needs to hook up with their community of resources. Helping clients do this is a really good way to achieve the third *GC* step of creating a generative COACH state. The illustration shows a version of the 6-step method by which this can be done. Let's explore it via a case example.

---

1   And in that tradition, the three positive connections are Buddha (center), dharma (positive intention), and sangha (resource field).

Steps in Community of Resources

1. Open a COACH field

2. Identify positive intention and layout timeline

3. Develop community of resources

    a. Identify several resources

    b. Organize them in a spatial field around the self

    c. Connect with each member of the creative team to form a generative self

4.   Explore action steps on the timeline

5.   Use resource community to transform obstacles

6.   Make a commitment to bring the changes into real life.

Steve and his community of resources

Dana was a software engineer for a mid-sized software development company. She loved her work, except for the monthly presentations she had to make to the tech team. She was sure that "everybody" thought her lectures were so "boring and dry and stupid" that they hated having to sit through them. Dana carried an Asperger's syndrome condition that she used to explain her social awkwardness, but also had quite a quirky sense of humor. Her goal was precise and clear: She wanted to do a better job in her presentations, and maybe even enjoy doing it. It felt like a good place to find a community of resources.

Steps 1 and 2: Open a Coach Field/ Identify a Positive Intention

In the initial conversation, Dana was very clear about her intention of improving her presentation performance and experience. But it was extremely difficult for her to develop any kind of a COACH state. Her body was locked with chronic tension and her verbal mind would dominate, insisting that she just needed to know what to do. My attempts—both verbal and nonverbal—to help her ease into a COACH field seemed to make her more anxious.

We want to point out how common this is. Sixty years of research shows that any method works only about 60% of the time. With those 40% of clients with whom basic technique does not work, top-performing practitioners are able to succeed by feedback-based improvisations (see Miller et al, 2013). As we move into the more advanced aspects of generative coaching, this is crucial to know.

The conversation was definitely in that "all basic techniques fail" space. The adage seemed apt: *When you find yourself in a hole, stop digging.* Time to regroup into COACH and pray for a Plan B. It seemed clear that connecting through the "upstairs" verbal mind wasn't working, so going "downstairs" through the somatic channel seemed like a good alternative. Attuning to my somatic center and hers, I became curious as to what might directly touch her nonverbal mind.

Food? *No.* food was just for biological maintenance. Music? *No. Loud noises overwhelmed her.* Friends? *No, I have no friends.* Dropping deeper into COACH, I asked my creative mind to let something, anything, come to mind. *An image of her gardening floated up. (Thank you!)* I shared it with her, and something shifted: She shyly affirmed her love for gardening. (She had a garden on her apartment balcony.) *Here was a portal to her COACH state.*

Not surprisingly, talking made it disappear. We needed a different somatic base. Summoning the ancestral energies—tenderness, playfulness, seriousness—I asked her if she talked to her plants while gardening. The room brightened: *Yes, I do.* Did the plants talk back? *Yes, of course.*

This illuminated a passageway into her "secret garden" of COACH. I gently suggested we move down to the ground, so she could more directly describe her experience of gardening. That shy but vulnerable look again appeared, and then we both sat on the floor, imagining sitting in her garden.

I asked her to introduce the various plants and flowers to me, which she did with pleasure. (She had never done so with another person. She was an "only child," describing her mother as a depressed accountant, and her father as an emotionally distant engineer. She had no memories of play or laughter or affection in her family.) We talked about how she cared for the plants and what kind of conversations they had. In doing so, her COACH state came into bloom.

I reflected how her state had shifted. She nodded but said it was hard to talk about. Moving back to her goal of becoming a better speaker, I suggested she needed some creative support, with a gentle smile pointing out that clearly her "super-reasonable" engineer self couldn't get the job done on her own. She looked intrigued but then anxious, starting to shift back into her verbal CRASH mind. I gently interrupted, suggesting that maybe this was the kind of conversation that she could have with her gardening "chums."

Step 3: Developing a "Community of Resources"

We were definitely working "on the creative edge" now, where careful attention to nonverbal resonance is needed to stay connected to a generative conversation. Sharing the "secret garden" space with Dana, I guided her to feel her hands in the dirt, making connection with the earth and the plants with her own whole being. (These are actual somatic movements that coach and client are both doing.) I then suggested that she ask the garden:

> *What kind of creative resources might help me give a great presentation?*

I suggested that upon asking the question, she just continue (in her imagination) to work in the garden, enjoying the dirt and smell and colors of her conversations. And within those experiences, to let any images come.

She did so, then suddenly looked intrigued and puzzled, followed by a burst of laughter. Two images had popped into her mind: the dog Toto (from the *Wizard of Oz*), and a "court jester" leaning against the wall with a whimsical smile. *Welcome!*

She was astonished by these images. First, by the fact that she closed her eyes and a dog and clown showed up. (There's got to be some joke here: An engineer, a dog, and a clown walk into a bar...) Second, it was *her* imagination that produced these resources... *Hers!* She had labored through life under the dark belief cloud that she had no imagination, but here it was: *She* had a creative mind.

The next challenge was to bring them into her creative team. I invited Dana to sense the spatial locations for each resource. (The general preference is for them to flank the client to maintain connection as they move into action.) We were still kneeling on the ground, and she pointed out the dog close on her left side, and the jester leaning whimsically against the garden wall to her right. I asked her to first sense her self, then move over and become the dog, then move over into the somatic model of the jester.

I would model each connection, then invite her to try it out. As a dog lover, it was easy for me to become Toto, barking and panting with delight, and then the playful bemused jester. This modeling by the coach is often very helpful, as it energetically opens the space for the client, while giving the coach 'insider information.'

I was impressed by how willing and able Dana was to do these experiential identifications. Definitely shy, but like a child at the circus or fair. She seemed especially thrilled to bark like a dog, and "nuzzle up."

Steps 4 and 5: Action Plans and Obstacles

Now it was time to rehearse how this "band of three" might collaborate on a great performance. We stood up and laid out a timeline, culminating in her giving a great presentation three weeks into the future. The members of the creative team were ready for action: Dana in the middle, Toto close by on her left, and the jester leaning against the wall.

Dana was asked to focus on the goal and sense her best strategy for achieving it. Predictably, she looked tense and "up in her head." She was then coached into the position of Toto, where she could sense Dana's presence and offer any support. I joined her down on the ground as Toto, barking and nuzzling the (imagined) Dana with a loving "mammal" connection. It was such a delightful pattern interruption for Dana, and we laughed in moving between Dana's super seriousness to Toto's loving playfulness.

A similar deep opening was found when Dana moved between her mirthless engineer mode and the relaxed comical state of the jester. It was a beautiful awakening of a generative state of tenderness, seriousness, and playfulness. You could feel how each time these energies integrated, a generative self was born.

The team slowly walked the timeline, unfolding in her imagination a path for achieving her goal. At the goal state, she picked up Toto in her arms and raised her in a celebratory gesture. I asked her to take a few moments and let her "community mind" of Dana/Toto/jester "memorize" that experience, and commit to taking it into the world.

We met for one more session. We moved through the experiential connections in her "community of resources" and rehearsed further how she could activate them during her talk.

She came back the following week so happy. It worked! On the way to the presentation, her old anxiety began to surface, but then so did the irrepressible affection of Toto barking and nuzzling. As she looked up, she saw the twinkling eyes of the jester. The three of them worked to give an exceptional presentation. People stayed afterwards to talk further and share their gratitude. A good time was had by all.

We talked about this as the beginning of a long next chapter in her life. I mentioned how old CRASH states are never erased, just replaced by better alternatives. And how we use the suffering of the old CRASH patterns and the joy of the new COACH patterns as equal ways to move forward in our growth and development. I suggested that Toto and the jester have the last word in the conversation, which was a delight for all.

Summary

The isolated ego is no match for the great challenges of life. Make friends with the voice that tells you, *you're not enough*. Let it remind you that you can only succeed in connection with resources. *We get by with a little help from our friends.*

We've explored in this chapter how the wisdom of our ancestors brings us the archetypal energies of **tenderness, positive fierceness,** and **playfulness**. In a CRASH state, they become the negative energies that haunt and attack us; in a COACH state, they are core resources for a creative life.

We also explored what it means to develop and make practical use of the "community of resources" needed for sustainable creativity. Creative wholeness has many dimensions—courage, centering, confidence, and so forth—and we need to find the beings and places in the world that help us to develop deep sustained connection to these dimensions. They are our community of resources.

May these two core dimensions join the *three positive connections* (center, intention, resources) we laid down as the prototype method for this important third step of generative coaching. And may you have a lot of success and fun in integrating them into your skill set.

Start close in

Start right now
take a small step
you can call your own
don't follow
someone else's
heroics, be humble
and focused,
start close in,
don't mistake
that other
for your own.
Start close in,
don't take
the second step
or the third,
start with the first
thing
close in,
the step
you don't want to take.

~ David Whyte

Chapter 5

Step 4
Take Action

Now we come to the all-important step: *How do you translate your dream into a sustainable reality?* We start with the realization that no matter how amazing the coaching session was, nothing has really changed yet. The session work opens *possibilities*, the *actual* reality happens after the session. Successful coaching occurs on the borderline between activating inner potential and committed, feedback-based outer action.

To create sustainable outcomes, it's important to move between a deep passionate positive intention—e.g., *I will create this new outcome*—and a series of sensory-based "stepping stones" for how this can happen. Each complements the other to forge a creative result. In GC1, we touched upon three main methods: (1) **storyboards** that create a visual representation of the narrative structure of a process; (2) **timelines** that lay out in time and space the series of specific steps to be taken; and (3) "to do" lists and daily diaries of commitments, actions, results, and revisions.

Their success depends on *disciplined flow*: the discipline to create an effective plan, and the *flow* to unfold it in feedback-sensitive fluid ways. There's an old saying in sports: *The game plan works until the game begins.* No matter how prepared we are, reality never unfolds quite the way we imagined. Another saying from martial arts: *Expect nothing, be ready for anything.* So planning and preparation is crucial, but so is our generative ability to creatively respond to whatever shows up.

We're not looking for the "one true" map that is repeated blindly each time, but a multi-dimensional deep structure that is practiced dozens, even hundreds of times. The 6-step GC model is an example of this. Hopefully, the more you practice it, the more you realize that there are infinite ways to apply it. Each session provides a new opportunity to discover a different way to apply the six steps.

To understand the practical nature of *disciplined flow*, let's start with the deep structure for a timeline/storyboard.

> **Step 1:** Open a COACH field
>
> **Step 2:** Identify positive intention
>
> **Step 3:** Layout timeline, step to starting point, develop the three positive connections (intention, center, somatic model).
>
> **Step 4:** Slowly move through timeline, identifying a specific sequence of actions to be taken at each step.
>
> **Step 5:** Identify and transform obstacles along the way.
>
> **Step 6:** Complete and review the timeline journey, commit to action, go do it with multiple revisions.

This is a general level of mapping, the sort you can hold in your mind as you do a coaching session. Each time, these steps need to be "filled in" with more specific applications. For example, we focused in the last two chapters on the three archetypal energies of *tenderness, fierceness, and playfulness*. Moving between these three creative states might be especially helpful in walking a timeline.

DISCIPLINED FLOW

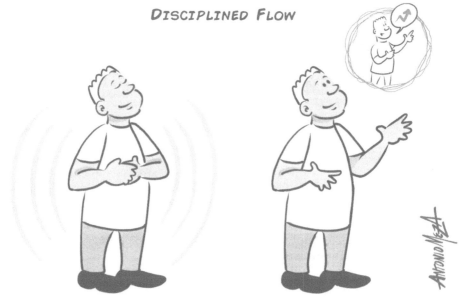

Step 1: Open a COACH field   Step 2: Identify positive intention

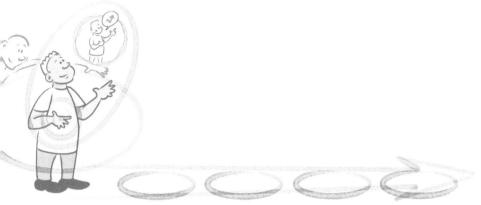

Step 3: Layout the timeline and develop the three positive connections

Step 4: Identify sequence of actions in the timeline

Step 5: Identify and transform obstacles along the way

Step 6: Complete and review the timeline journey, commit to action.

The Disney Strategy: Dreamer, Realist, and Positive Critic

Another triad of creativity modes is Robert's modeling of the creative patterns of Walt Disney:

- **Dreamer** — Imagining what is possible

- **Realist** — Planning how to reach goals

- **Critic** — Evaluating the plan according to key values and looking for problems and missing links

As we discussed in *GC1*, the first mode of *Dreamer* is unbounded imagination. You sense a possibility and let multiple representations of it develop. *Wow, I'm excited about this idea. Maybe it would look like this… or maybe THIS… or maybe that…* Such open curiosity is crucial to unfold a new vision or possible reality. It's where a generative change begins, but also is crucial when the imagination has run dry, or when you are in an "I don't know" state. This is most like a COACH field: you let go of all preconceptions and maps, and swim for a while in the quantum ocean of infinite possibilities.

But at some point, attention needs to shift to the *Realist* level where you say: *From among the infinite possibilities, I select THIS ONE as the most promising way to make the dream real.* Attention narrows to a more specific thinking that includes people, places, timing, sequences, etc. It is of course the complement to the dreamer, they work hand-in-hand. The goal here is to develop a sort of prototype model to guide the effective implementation of a vision.

Once a rough prototype is developed, the *positive Critic* becomes important. Many people think of the critic in a negative way, someone who tears things apart, thinks people or ideas are stupid, etc. But the *positive Critic* is someone who passionately believes in the project and has this sense, *we can do this better. We have to continue to change, revise, improve, reorganize, streamline, add, etc.*

The *positive Critic* is the difference between mediocrity and excellence. Intense questioning and an insatiable commitment to improvement is the difference that makes a difference. Again, the core position of the positive critic is:

We can make this even better.

These are three interconnected levels of creativity. But remember, there are the constructive (COACH) and destructive (CRASH) versions of each mode. Without a COACH state, the Dreamer is just lost in fantasy. The Realist in CRASH is a bureaucrat – there's no spark anymore. The Critic without COACH is very unpleasant and destructive. So, in terms of creativity, the COACH state is the primary platform, and then the *Dreamer*, the *Realist* and the *Critic* are a second level.

Integrating the Dreamer, Realist, and Critic modes on a Timeline Process

We use these Disney modes as a central method in coaching clients on timeline/storyboard work. We discuss the importance of *open imagination and curiosity (Dreamer), reality-based practical focus (Realist), and positive editing and improvement (Critic)*. And then we suggest that each be used in exploring how to forge a creativity map. So now Step 4 becomes more specific:

1. Coach field

2. Intention

3. Generative state

4. Walk the timeline

    a. Dreamer state

    b. Realist state

    c. Positive Critic state

    d. Generative state (integration of three modes)

    e. Variations

5. At "finish line," look back at success path(s). Commitment, gratitude.

In this version, the first three steps are used to create a generative state focused on a specific goal, including laying out a timeline. Then the client attunes to a creativity mode and slowly walks the timeline to sense different action steps that might be taken. This is repeated for each of the three modes—*Dreamer, Reality, and Positive Critic*—and then for a "generative self" that integrates the three modes.

One simple way to activate a creativity mode:

1. Select one of the creative modes (e.g., Dreamer);

2. Identify a representative of that mode (e.g., *Who would be a really good model of someone with creative vision and imagination?*);

3. Imagine the representative standing next to you on the timeline;

4. Find a somatic model and resonance to be in rapport with the representative;

5. Use this connection to walk the timeline, identifying step-by-step ways to achieve the goal.

To make this have lasting value, the coach's primary commitment is helping the client to stay in a productive COACH state. This requires a lot of coaching skill, as most clients lose their COACH state many times in the process. They might get too much in their head, or run into obstacles, or move too fast. For sustainable generative change, we're not trying to force the client into the box of generative coaching. We're looking to adapt the GC methods to join and support each unique client pattern, "upgrading" the system to a generative COACH level.

To illustrate this, let's look a session with a 35-year old school teacher, Leonard. He wanted help in succeeding in a budding intimacy relationship. As you will note, the movement between different creativity modes followed his state changes.

Setting a positive intention

S: *Hi Leonard, welcome.*

L: *Thanks, I'm happy to be here.*

S: *So, let's take a few moments to identify what would be your intention or goal here today. If there was one thing you would love to creatively change in your life, what would that be?*

L: *To manifest myself fully.*

S: *And if you were able to manifest yourself fully, what would you be able to specifically create? If we were to look into the future—say, a month or six months or a year from now, what would we be seeing?*

L: *I would like to achieve an intimacy relationship in my personal life.*

S: *Yeah. Are you in an intimacy relationship?*

(Leonard hesitates, then nods.)

L: *Yes.*

S: *Is it a long-term relationship?*

L: *Hopefully so.* (laughs)

S: *Okay. So, there's some emerging relationship?* (smiles)

(Leonard nods, smiles, then looks a bit apprehensive.)

S: *How long have you been with this person?*

L: *About 3 months…*

S: *May I ask their name?*

L: *Lily.*

S: *Great. Nice name. And how long would you like to be in this relationship with Lily?*

L: (smiles) *Forever…*

(Both S and L laugh.).

S: *Ok, great. So, am I understanding you'd like some confidence and capacity to nurture this into a long-term relationship?*

L: *Yes, very much so.*

S: *I hear you. I feel that. I see that. And to that place inside of you, I say,* **welcome!** *I'd love to support you in that.*

L: *Thank you.*

S: *My pleasure. And so, just to deepen your connection with that intention, I'd like to invite you to tune in… and sense… that place of your deepest longing, your deepest dream… feel where its center is in your body… in terms of that hope, that longing…*

(Leonard closes his eyes, touches his heart, and slowly opens his arms outward into the world.)

L: *Here it is…* (Shows somatic model)

S: *Awesome.* (To the audience). *I don't know if you could see, his chest starts to open there.* (S touches chest and opens arms outward. Leonard nods, relaxes.) *Remember, as a coach, we want to bring tenderness and kindness, and seriousness and playfulness. So, when somebody is really shy, or it's a delicate, vulnerable area, we want to touch those places with loving kindness.*

(Leonard continues moving his hands.)

S: *So, I wonder if there's some words of intention that go with that center and somatic model…* **What would be really great for me to be able experience in this intimacy relationship is…**"

L: *What I really want to create in this relationship is genuine love and affection.*

S: *Great...* (Mirrors Leonard's movements). *You really want to create a relationship of love and affection... I feel that. I send you lots of "big brother" support for that. Welcome!*

L: (smiles, looks vulnerable, nods). *Thanks. I feel that.*

S: *So, Leonard, let's see what you can do to make that happen. We've been talking about creating action plans on timelines, and also how this creative process is part "dreamer", part "realist", and part "positive critic."*

L: (nods)

S: (Takes a few minutes to help Leonard lay out timeline, make positive connections with center, intention, and resources.)

The Dreamer (Deepak Chopra)

S: *And one thing I'd like to suggest that I think you might find really helpful and interesting, is that each time you walk the timeline, you bring a resource along with you, someone who can model, remind, and guide you into your best state.*

Let's start with how to tap into your creative imagination and allow that part of you to unfold a timeline sequence.... I'm wondering, is there somebody who is a good model of that for you? Somebody who really is a great representative of open imagination?

L: (pauses for a few moments, then smiles). *Well, the image of Deepak Chopra popped up.* (laughs). *I didn't expect that!.*

S: (Smiles). *Wow, so when we put out the invitation for a creative dreamer to join the conversation, Deepak Chopra answered the call. That's interesting! I hope it's ok to say to Deepak, **welcome! Thanks for joining us!***

L: (smiles, nods). *Welcome, Deepak...*

S: *And I'd like to invite Deepak to be your escort on the Dreamer timeline. You can feel his presence next to you, feel the connection to his Dreamer spirit...* (Leonard begins to slowly move, repeating his arms extending outwards)... *and as you feel that connection, take a first step forward and sense... in my deepest imagination, what images or songs or movements come to represent a first step I can take to deepen this intimacy relationship?*

L: (with eyes closed, begins a slow, fluid dance movement, taking a step forward)

S: (Mirroring Leonard's movements, right alongside him.) **One small step for Leonard, one giant step for men in intimacy relationships.** (joke)... *And tell me what you become aware there?*

L: (smiles). *I saw Deepak's face, and his voice saying, you create your reality...* **infinite possibilities!!**

S: That's right... so isn't it nice to know that each time you start an intimacy process, you can feel that positive presence of Deepak reminding you of that... And as you continue to feel that rhythm... feel that somatic model representing bringing positive intimacy in the relationship... seeing and feeling the presence of Deepak Chopra as an ally... let yourself take a next step...

(This process continued for three more timeline steps. At each successive step, Leonard reported experiencing: *a crying baby being held and comforted by Leonard; two dogs playing in a grassy field; Leonard and his sweetheart laughing together.*

At end of the Dreamer timeline, Leonard is invited to sense the steps he just took, breathe them into integration, then move back to the "starting gates" for a second round, this time in the Realist mode.)

Walking in a timeline with multiple possibilities: a crying baby, two dogs playing, and his sweetheart laughing with him.

The Realist (Barack Obama)

S: *So, ready for another round?*

L: *Yes.*

S: *Great. In this second round I want to invite you to tune into your Realist mode, to really focus on the specific things you can actually do with your sweetheart when you're with her. Ok?*

L: (Tenses, shrinks a bit, looks insecure.). *Well, that's easier said than done. I'm pretty good in my fantasies, I'm pretty safe in my imagination, but something happens when I'm actually connecting to people, especially in an intimacy relationship.*

S: *That's great to know, that in reality connections, you get overwhelmed.*

L: *Yeah, pretty much.*

S: *To that part of you that feels overwhelmed and insecure, I'd like to say, welcome. And also point out that this is the place where your resources are most needed. So, I wonder, when you think about a good representative of a Realist person who can do intimacy, who comes to mind?*

L: (Smiles) *Barack Obama. I think he's so cool, and I really admire his relationship with his wife.*

S: *Wow, let's welcome President Obama. Welcome, Mr. President, welcome!* (smiles and makes movement of welcoming Mr. Obama). *And I know you are a very busy man, but this wonderful young man has requested the honor of your support as a resource for him. Will you help Leonard?* (S turns to Leonard). *What does he say?*

L: (smiles). *He says in that kind-hearted, casual way, that he would be happy to do that.*

S: *Great. So let yourself imagine Barack Obama standing next to you on your journey of intimacy. And wow, he's probably a much more powerful big brother than I could ever be.* (S and L laugh.). *What do you become aware of now?*

L: *Well, actually, his wife is standing with him, they're holding hands, smiling at me.*

S: *Wow, we may have to charge you extra for that.* (Both laugh) *Two for one, that's great! So, let's tune to the steps of the timeline.... Feel the support of Barack and Michele Obama, a beautiful couple to guide and support you... and feel your own somatic presence, as a young man committed to finding his path of intimacy... and then when you're ready, let yourself take a first step forward...*

L: (Goes to move, freezes, looks distressed.)

S: (With gentle voice) *Let's pause... breathe... center... no need to do anything... come back to COACH... and feel Barack Obama's voice speaking, perhaps, offering a simple support. And what happens now?*

L: *I just feel overwhelmed...*

S:(Gently) *That's good to know that the vulnerable part comes up as you go to do intimacy. And to that part that is experiencing overwhelm,* **welcome**. *I'm sure that makes sense. Often it means that you're asking too much, going too fast... So, let's take it as a suggestion to* **slow down**... *hear Mr. Obama's voice, what does he say?*

L: *He agrees with you. He says, no pressure, just be yourself, it's ok to feel vulnerable.*

S: *Well, that doesn't surprise me. Let's both take in those words of wisdom, and breathe... and slow down... and the thing about the Realist,*

it's looking at simple details, things that are real... like your breath going in and out... like your feet touching the ground... like thinking, **what's one small thing that would be a good first step?**

L: *I saw the image of the Obamas holding hands, and then I felt and saw myself extend my hand out to Lily (his sweetheart)...* (Leonard slows down, breathes, relaxes, smiles.)

S: *That's great. No need for lots of words, no big plans, no major demands... just holding hands... That's a really good first step... just holding hands... small chunks, slow down, simple actions... holding hands... and what how does Barack respond to that?*

L: *He smiles and nods and winks... as he holds up his hand connection with Michelle.*

S: *That's what resources are for! And as you feel that touch of the hand... the smile and support of the Obamas... let yourself take another step as the Realist. What do you notice here?*

L: (Leonard moves forward a little step, again looks like he enters CRASH state. Mumbles:) *Communication. Just communication.*

S: (Gently) *Communicate what specifically?*

(Leonard shrugs shoulders, indicates resignation.)

S: (Gently). *Great. Here's one of the most important steps in the whole process. This is where you really get to connect to your deepest capacity to love. It feels like it's been sort of locked in the basement for a long time. I'd like to say to that presence, **Welcome. Welcome. You're so important to the process.***

(At such CRASH points, the coach welcomes whatever is there, and helps the client connect to COACH resources to be able to positively integrate it. Steve does this by connecting Leonard to (1) his own body, (2) his resource of Barack Obama, and (3) to Steve's human support. Leonard finds that the intimacy path activated his wounded child, and the COACH support allows him to welcome it as an integral part of his present intimacy self.)

S: *And from there, Leonard, connecting first to yourself... to that vulnerable place inside of you... to the kind big brother support of Barack Obama... as you look at Linda from this place, what is it you want to say?*

L: (slowly) *I want to say to Linda: I love you, but it takes me a while to get there sometimes. (Looks vulnerable but stays connected)*

S: *That's great... I feel that... and what do Barack and Michele say?*

L: (smiles) *They look so happy and proud of me!*

S: *Yeah, you got lots of support now for that vulnerability and that commitment to intimacy... and hey, since it takes your vulnerable side some time to get there, I guess that means you've got time on your hands, to do a few other things, right?* (smiles)

L: (laughs). *I guess so...*

S: *Well, while you let that really vulnerable part of you take his time behind the scenes, why don't you skip ahead... and you might bring Barack and Deepak with you... and see... hell, just for the fun of it, what I'd like to do with Linda is...* (Steve models this with child-like playfulness, dancing around. He coaxes Leonard, who after several minutes starts moving freely. With these playful somatic movements, he moves through several more timeline steps, discovering images of bringing flowers to Linda, talking with her about his family pain, and making videos for her.).

(So, we see quite a different response in the Realist mode than in the Dreamer mode. Lots of CRASH in the Realist, which means it's got lots of unintegrated creative power to welcome and integrate. Shifting to a gentle, then playful energy, allows that wounded part to be welcomed into the solution self.)

At the end of the second timeline, Steve asks Leonard to pause, notice learnings, then return to starting point.

S: *Wow, that was interesting! Time for one more, perhaps… Are you up for it?*

L: *Yes, definitely.*

**Walking in a timeline supported by his mentor/archetype of the "Realist":
bringing flowers, talking about his family pain, recording videos.**

The Positive Critic (Bruce Lee)

S: *Well, now we come to that part of our creative self that is responsible for rejecting, changing, editing, rearranging, cutting out, revising. We call this the Positive Critic. Anything you think in this intimacy path you especially want to edit?*

L: *I want to let go of my insecurity and fear.*

S: *And replace it with what?*

L: (Pauses). *Well, I want to keep my ground when I feel criticized.*

S: *Great. That makes sense. And if you were to let yourself ponder who might be a good representative of that critic or editor... just notice who shows up this time.*

L: (Laughs). *Bruce Lee.*

S: *Wow, you have good taste! Bruce Lee has been one of my heroes since I started martial arts almost 50 years ago!* (S somatically models Bruce Lee, with his playful movements, sounds, and fierce eyes. L mirrors him back.)

And what do you especially like about Bruce Lee as a model?

L: *Well, he never backs down, but he's very playful, and has such powerful grace, and sometimes is just very serious.*

S: *Yes, a good male model, I agree. And what about that represents something you didn't have at a younger age, that you want to have now as you go forward with positive intimacy?*

L: (Looks young, vulnerable). *My family was pretty violent, there was a lot of yelling, and I really got beaten down. It made me insecure and unable to communicate well.*

S: *Yeah, I know that feeling.* (The two men silently connect.). *So now you're building a different family, with Dreamers like Deepak, loving Realists like Barack, and fierce positive critics that wag their fingers "no", like Bruce Lee.* (s\Silent connection.). *That's really good to know… I'm happy for you. (Silent connection)*

So, shall we set up the timeline with Bruce?

L: *Yeah, let's do it.* (Looks like he's pulling himself together into a more committed, mature presence.)

S: *And for this one, I suggest that not only might you imagine Bruce Lee to your side, but this image just came to me of YOU being Bruce Lee… you moving, and sounding, like Bruce. Did you ever do this privately, at home?*

L: (Laughs). *Yes, especially when I was a teenager.*

S: *Me too, and long after I was a teenager… Like maybe yesterday.* (They both laugh.). *What do you think?*

L: *I think that would be great.* (Steve and Leonard now exchange a few Bruce Lee movements, as if sparring with each other, both laughing.)

S: *And so, let's move onto that timeline one more time… And sense, Leonard, how much you are really, really committed to developing a positive intimacy relationship, hopefully with Linda. Slow down… feel it… let it be deep in your center. And from there sense the delight in discovering that spirit of Bruce Lee can guide you in some steps you need to take in that regard. So, you ready?*

L: *Yes, definitely.*

S: *Ok, so let yourself find a movement like Bruce Lee, then let it bring you forward into one movement, into a first step of saying: **As a first step, the dragon enters to say***… (Steve models this, jumping around, leaping forward with a fierce statement. He then bows to L, and nonverbally signals that it's his turn. L is a bit shy, but then he breaks into the free movement.)

L: *Whaaaa*… (Bruce Lee sound). *A first thing I need to do is*… *say to my family, **I don't want to be the victim anymore, I want to have my own life!!*** (He looks very intense and vulnerable, mostly centered.)

S: (Nods, speaks seriously but gently). *That's great. that's it, Leonard. Now finish it off with a few really good Bruce Lee moves*…

(Steve somatically models Bruce Lee, and Leonard joins him, the two playfully fierce.).

(Steve is now thinking of Muhammed Ali, and starts somatically modeling Ali, dancing and prancing.). *And how about inviting Muhammed Ali onto the team*… *I float like a butterfly, but I sting like a bee!!* (S dances around like Ali. With a little prodding, L mirrors that as well.)

S: *That's so cool, Leonard. Really great. And so let yourself find that positive male fierceness*…. *open hearted*… *playful*… *indomitable*… *centered*… *And feel with that fierce protective Critic, letting yourself speak no voice but your own*… *walk a few more steps.*

L: (Makes somatic model of his arm extended forward, like a sword, begins to slowly walk through the timeline. This time he finds additional images*: finding a fierce silent center when his inner critic attacks; dancing like Bruce Lee when he feels intimidated; and a somatic model of one hand on his heart, the other extending forward...*)

S: *It's good. Feels good, huh?*

L: (Nods). *Really good...*

S: *You look great.*

(To the audience) *So, just by exploring these, you can begin to get a sense of what a person's relationship is to each of these three core parts.*

So, we'll go back to the beginning, and we'll put that together.

(They walk back to the beginning.)

Walking in a timeline supported by his mentor/archetype of the "Positive Critic": finding a fierce silent center; dancing like Bruce Lee; one hand in heart, one hand forward.

Integration and Future Orientation

S: *As a way to integrate, let's just walk through the kata or choreograph of this process.* (With each step, S models and invites L to mirror)... *Let's begin with a COACH field...* (somatic model)... *then the intention...* (somatic model)... **Each day, I grow more mature and committed to a healthy intimacy relationship...** (nonverbal, somatic modeling)... **And I feel all the community of mature resources to guide... remind... support, and provide examples...**

(Dreamer) Deepak Chopra... infinite possibilities... reminding you of the need for creative imagination... (somatic model, smiles, playful)...

(Realist) Barack Obama... a gentle realist... reminding you... slow down... simplicity, simplicity, simplicity.... small things... stay centered and present... first connection with yourself... then to others... a way to begin to integrate, kindness and kinship, respect for women... centered...

(Positive Critic) Bruce Lee... the dancing critic... not allowing abuse... fiercely cutting through intimidation... centering... positive self-defense... celebration of the body.... Rising above abuse... centered... centered... a deep intimacy with your heart and soul... a deep commitment to the daily practice...

And most of all, you... Leonard... a man awakening to his positive intimacy... a man healing, helping... becoming... each day...

And so just note what you've created here... feel how each day you can practice this timeline: What can I do today to further develop my intimacy? A question for the ages... And

moving through that connection... starting with yourself... center, positive intention, resources... then taking a step at a time.... and remembering... positive imagination, infinite possibilities... practical reality, small steps, staying connected... fierce changes and revisions, positive warrior... and feeling all of them integrated, more each day, as you walk the steps each day...

And looking back on the paths you've begun to lay down, let yourself center... make any commitments or vows you'd like to make... thank all the beings that support you on this path... (pause)... and then, as a completion, let yourself find a somatic model and voice to celebrate... Yes, I did it.... one voice saying... infinite possibilities... another, Yes, we can!... another, just the sound of the dancing dragon... and most important, your own voice saying... Yes ... yes... yes...

(Leonard moves and smiles and bows... for several minutes. Then turns to S, and bows). *Thank you!*

S: (Hugs L). *Thank you too, brother. Thanks for sharing a core piece of your life journey. Thanks for being a student of yourself, and a teacher for all of us.* (Hand extends to other people in the room.). *How many of you got some therapy from Leonard here today?*

People raise their hands, shower Leonard with support, give a standing ovation. Leonard is clearly deeply touched. Steve walks over, throws his arm around Leonard, and says: *Now the work begins.*

Using the Disney Model on a Timeline

1) SET AN INTENTION

2) IDENTIFY A REPRESENTATIVE OF DREAMER AND WALK THE TIMELINE

3) IDENTIFY A REPRESENTATIVE OF REALIST AND WALK THE TIMELINE

4) FIND REPRESENTATIVE FOR POSITIVE CRITIC AND WALK THE TIMELINE

5) INTEGRATE AND COMMIT

General Discussion

This is but one of the many ways that storyboard/timelines can be used in generative coaching. In the "disciplined flow" of GC, we see the method as a simple clear prototype for unfolding a path to a desired reality, but one that will be expressed in many unique ways. Remember, generative sustainability depends on including all dimensions of a performance holon—the goal, the present state, resources, obstacles, contextual conditions, etc. So, the actual performance is a sort of collective improvisation organized around a general blueprint.

In the above example, we see the importance of activating the different creativity modes of *Dreamer* (open imagination), *Realist* (practical application), and *Positive Critic* (continuous revision and improvement). Each is an essential skill for sustainable creativity. Like Leonard, most people are strong in one area, but not in another. Leonard was very comfortable in his Dreamer, but quickly contracted in the Realist. This was taken as feedback to "chunk down" to a slower pace and smaller steps, and also activate multiple resources—e.g., to somatic centering, the connection to the coach, and connection to his "Barack Obama" resource.

In moving through the timeline (in the session and afterwards), Leonard began to sense how his old "intimacy maps" were primarily negative: an abusive father as a male model, a violent relationship between his parents, his family-learned self-criticism, no positive support, etc. It was especially important for him to realize there was nothing wrong or deficient about him, he had just inherited some painful CRASH patterns from his family. Practicing the timeline over many weeks allowed him to identify these CRASH dimensions and replace them with COACH representations.

Running into these debilitating CRASH points is not a question of if, but when. It's rare that what brings a client into coaching is merely a lack of skill or knowledge; almost always there are unresolved CRASH points that dissociate a person from their hard-earned skills. There are many tell-tale signs of CRASH: emotional reactivity, losing focus, stuckness in some experience, somatic locking, etc. At these points, coaching shifts from "moving forward into a positive future" to reconnecting to the COACH state. The generative coach can quickly run through the six steps—opening a COACH field, positive intention, the three positive connections, chunking down into sub-steps, welcoming obstacles—as a way of sensing which dimensions of the performance holon need to be integrated for creative flow to resume. (Remember, each step contains all the other steps.) This means that each session will be unique and very illuminating, for both coach and client.

I DON'T WANT TO BE THE VICTIM ANYMORE, I WANT TO HAVE MY OWN LIFE!

Using the "time-line" technique in order to move into action, and supported by your own representatives of the three archetypal energies: Dreamer, Realist and Positive Critic.

The general methods of timeline and storyboard are used in virtually every high-performance field. Athletes visualize and rehearse their performance endless times to prepare for a great performance. Coaching during a competition usually involves returning to the core plan; and afterwards, the match is reviewed many times to analyze how to improve. Training involves using the performance maps under many conditions, so you develop the confidence that, whatever may happen, you have the skill and resilience to creatively respond. This is what we're looking to do in generative coaching. We don't want to give a client some rigid map, we want to support them in "learning to learn" coherent, flexible strategies for success.

This means that the session work is a beginning, not an end. In Step 6, we usually review what happened and ask clients to identify and commit to 2-3 actions for that week, and to keep records. We'll see in Chapter 7 how these homework commitments play out in many ways. Sometimes clients "forget" or "didn't have time" to do them. Other times they start and get overwhelmed or sidetracked; or unanticipated conditions or events occur. *Each outcome is welcomed as positive feedback about what is needed for further improvement.*

As with all GC methods, the storyboard/timeline prototype is not a technique to impose upon the client, but a general map by which clients can "learn to learn" positive development. As the old saying goes: *Give a man a fish and you feed him for a day. Teach him how to fish and you feed him for a lifetime.*

With the timeline methods, we're supporting clients in learning how to productively make use of their deep commitment, hard work, and continuous learning. This evolves the confidence to live life with an open heart and curious mind. It reminds us of what we heard Milton Erickson so often say: *I don't know how that will happen, but I'm curious to find out!* This is the essence of generative learning, and the GC methods provide the base to make that a reality. As Deepak Chopra would say: *There are infinite possibilities.* Barack Obama would say: *Yes, we can!* And Bruce Lee would say: *Whaaaaaa!*

This being human is a guest house.
Every morning a new arrival.
A joy, a depression, a meanness,
some momentary awareness comes
as an unexpected visitor.
Welcome and entertain them all!
Even if they are a crowd of sorrows,
who violently sweep your house
empty of its furniture,
still, treat each guest honorably.
He may be clearing you out
for some new delight.
The dark thought, the shame, the malice.
meet them at the door laughing and invite them in.
Be grateful for whatever comes.
because each has been sent
as a guide from beyond.

– Rumi

Chapter 6
Step 5
Transforming Obstacles

Everywhere you go, problems are there to greet you. If you have a car, you'll have car problems. If you have an intimacy relationship, you'll have intimacy problems. If you work, you'll have work problems. Problems are an integral part of life, so it's no surprise that we consider them an essential, integral part of generative coaching. The question thus becomes: What is the best way to understand and relate to significant obstacles?

To answer that, let's consider what makes problems worse. In GC terms, we need look no further than the 4 Fs of the CRASH state: fight, flight, freeze, or fold. If you try to overpower your problems, they usually get worse. If you run away from them, they get worse. If you try to deal with them in some sort of frozen analysis paralysis, they get worse. And if you just numb out, they get worse.

When we add the fifth "F" of creative flow, we see what not only what resolves problems, but can transform them into the very resources needed to move forward in life. So, we say:

> *The problem is not the problem. Your relationship to the "problem" is the problem (or the solution).*

And:

> *The attempted solution becomes the problem.*

> *The problem is an unintegrated resource for the solution.*

To make sense of this, we want to first return to our 2-level model of experiential reality, to see how problems and resources share the very same archetypal root. CRASH relationships turn the root into a problem, while COACH relationships allow them to mature into human resources.

The Two-level Model of Experience

Our first home is the quantum field of collective consciousness. This field contains the ancestral history, organized around *archetypal patterns* of how to create human lives. Each archetypal pattern is a holographic representation of the countless ways that a core human challenge has been met. (By holographic we mean it's a not a fixed isolated image, but a spectral map that contains all possible forms of the pattern.) In GC, we give special emphasis to three such archetypal patterns: *tenderness*, *fierceness*, and *playfulness*.

Tenderness

Fierceness   **Playfulness**

This primary level is not especially active during mundane tasks, where you can just repeat what you've done before. But when you face a challenge that requires a new creative response, your *somatic center* opens the gateway to the creative unconscious. Through those channels stream ancestral patterns and energies to help you meet that challenge. *These experiences are not coming from your individual mind, but from the deeper collective consciousness. This is the first level of creativity, the "little circle."*

These core energies are not fully humanized. They are deep structures that can be instantiated in infinite possible ways, thereby allowing total creative freedom. It is the human connection to these archetypal patterns that give them their specific form and meaning. *This is the second level of creative reality, the "big circle."*

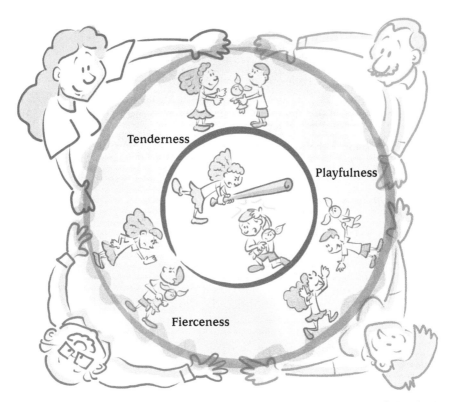

Tenderness

Playfulness

Fierceness

The family and adult community constitutes the "conscious mind" of the child.

This is perhaps easiest to see with children. They are clearly connected with the archetypal field of infinite possibilities. Life flows through them, each moment bringing a different experience. When my daughter was young, people would say: *She's so cute!* I would say: *Yes, she's that and much, much more.* Young children touch every experience in the world at least twice in a day, no wonder they sleep so deeply at night!

But from a human point of view, children are incomplete. They don't have the social-cognitive mind to shape and give meaning to their incredible energies. Thus, the family and adult community constitutes the "conscious mind" of the child. There's an old existentialist idea: Your first self-image comes from how you are mirrored back by others.

For example, let's imagine a young child who responds to her friend taking her toy by hitting the friend over the head with a bat. (I am not imagining this, I'm remembering it!). In an ideal world, the parent might say: *The force in this one is strong! But she needs a little help humanizing that fierceness.* You would then work with the child to value her fierceness, while also helping her develop ways to express it productively. This use of COACH connections is how an archetypal pattern becomes a positive human resource.

But let's imagine that girl swinging the bat is screamed at, told that nice girls never get angry, and warned to *never ever* do that again. She goes into CRASH, which turns the archetypal fierceness into a terrible negative experience that needs to be locked in the basement. She becomes a "good girl," chronically pleasant and agreeable. Meanwhile, she feels dead and empty inside, cut off from her soul fire.

Then at some point, something stirs. For example, she feels her calling as an investigative journalist, a job that requires a lot of fierceness. She states her positive intention as:

I really want to become a great journalist.

And her obstacle immediately appears:

But I really shut down when I have to call people on their bullshit.

(Or rather than being disconnected from it, she might be consumed by it):

But when I feel a person is lying, I blow up and totally go berserk.

The 2-level model allows us to see the "problem" as a *necessary resource* under the influence of a human curse. For the journalist, her "problem" carries the positive fierceness needed for deep commitment, healthy boundaries, speaking truth, and other "positive warrior" skills. *That's why it activates when she needs fierceness.* But because it appears in its negatively conditioned form, it is regarded only as a negative experience to be rejected. *The ensuing negative response to it unwittingly recreates it as the problem.* What we're looking to do in GC is creatively engage these "problems" in ways that they become resources.

Four Skill Sets for Transforming Negative Experiences

We want now to explore four skills sets needed to transform negative "problems" into positive resources.

1. Connecting to a COACH state.

2. Humanizing the negative experience

3. Relational "mantras"

4. Weaving positive resources

1. Connecting to a COACH State:

This is the core premise of GC: *generativity requires a COACH state*. A difficult experience becomes an impossible problem when held in a CRASH state. The journalist struggling to find an integrated fierceness would CRASH every time she touched it. It was forbidden fruit. You could see it in her body—inhibited breathing, locked shoulders, glazed eyes. And you could hear it in her words—*I have to overcome this problem; I have to stop being this way*. This hostility towards your experience is what makes it a terrible problem. As I like to say to clients: *Treat yourself like a dog. (Good boy! Good girl! Let's hug.)* You know with mammals, it's all about the kindness and nonverbal connection.

In generative coaching, the coach first develops their own COACH state. When a client hits CRASH, we assume it's activating in us at the same time; our mirror neurons work overtime. By recognizing it and shifting to a COACH state, we model what we are asking the client to do.

With the journalist, from my COACH connection I helped her find hers. It was *coaching girls in soccer*. That was used as a stable base to invite the unintegrated fierceness to a "tea ceremony" of generative healing.

2. Humanizing the Negative Experience

We usually use "negative it" language in relation to our "problems": *I just have to get rid of "it". It's a terrible thing.*

This dehumanizing language is the set-up for violence: For most people to do violence, they have to first represent the "other" as some inhuman monster or threat. Unfortunately, this is the language most used to describe "other than ego" experiences that touch people. Terms like "depression" and "panic" and "compulsions" don't exactly inspire respect and compassion, the very things needed for transformation. Generative change requires a language that "humanizes" what is perceived as the negative other. Three simple ways to do that: (1) providing home and shelter, (2) using human pronouns, and (3) sensing age.

Providing home and shelter

One humanizing question is: Where does it live (in your body)? When you are homeless, it's hard to be generative.

> *Where in your body do you feel the presence of that panic? When you feel depressed, where do you feel its center in your body?*

Often these questions are met with bewilderment:

> *I don't know… Everywhere… It's just there.*

By gently helping people find a COACH state, we can help them find the *felt sense* of the experience and give it sanctuary. In doing so, a person becomes more grounded and human. They can start a differentiated relationship with this **otherness**:

> *Oh, I'm here, and the other part of me lives there in my chest…*

It's not dissociation, it's positive differentiation. Only when the parts are differentiated is deeper integration possible. Sometimes we call this *inviting the obstacle to the tea ceremony*.

Personal pronouns

A second way to humanize negative otherness is through personal pronouns: We use "he" or "she" pronouns, rather than "it."

> *So there's a presence within you that right now is filled with anger.*

Or

> *"She" is filled with panic.*

Sometimes clients wonder what could this possibly mean:

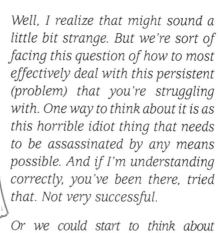

> *Well, I realize that might sound a little bit strange. But we're sort of facing this question of how to most effectively deal with this persistent (problem) that you're struggling with. One way to think about it is as this horrible idiot thing that needs to be assassinated by any means possible. And if I'm understanding correctly, you've been there, tried that. Not very successful.*

> *Or we could start to think about that deep presence that follows you around wherever you go...(gently) as some part of you that needs some connection... some way to be included.*

When done skillfully, this sort of conversation can be a game-changer: It allows the person to start a respectful and curious relationship to this otherness that lives so deeply within them. This is what allows transformation.

Age

A third humanizing language is to ask for ages associated with a difficult emotion:

> As you feel a connection to that place of sadness, I'd like to invite you to just let a number pop into your mind that represents an age for that feeling. Don't try to think it, just let it happen.

Often a person will be surprised by the number that pops in:

Client: *(Pause)... 6... (looks like some feeling is being touched)*

Coach: *So, when you tune to that sadness, the age of 6 pops up. That's interesting. And to whatever parts of you are connected to that, I just want to say, welcome!*

The point is not to have a person regress into childhood. On the contrary, it's to welcome forward any unintegrated "parts" or "ego states" that activate when a person connects to a needed resource.

Sensing it as a different age allows you to differentiate it from your present (competency-based) self:

> I am 40 years old, and this other part of me that panics is often around 6. She is a part of me, but not my deeper Self. I either invite her into all the resources of my present self, or we both get pulled back into the hellhole of my past. Hmmm, I wonder which is a better choice for me?

So, a client learns that when their old patterns activate, they don't regress. They take it as a cue to "welcome it forward" into the hard-earned competencies and connections of their present self. This core resource is unbound from its earlier negative base and bonded to the mature positive base of the present. This is one of the fundamental shifts in transforming negative experiences. As Jung used to say: *The first half of your life belongs to other people, the second half belongs to you.*

3. The Four Relational Mantras

In *GC1*, we discussed how unintegrated obstacles are positively welcomed into human connection via the four "relational mantras":

  1. That's interesting....

  2. I'm sure that makes sense...

  3. Something is trying to wake up (be heard, held or healed)

  4. Welcome!

THAT'S INTERESTING...
I'M SURE THAT MAKES SENSE...
SOMETHING IS TRYING TO WAKE UP
(BE HEARD, HELD OR HEALED)
WELCOME!

Of course, the nonverbal way in which these statements are expressed is the most important thing. They are not cliches to be mechanically parroted, but authentic expressions of human regard. We want to genuinely welcome each experience into the human community of positive regard and acceptance. We'll see below some further ways to skillfully use these "mantras."

4. Weaving Positive Resources

Persistent suffering reflects an isolation or "functional dissociation" of one identity part from its larger whole. Persistent problems have self-locking properties: when they activate, everything else disappears, and you're trapped inside of that "CRASH hell." You can see it in clients and feel it in yourself as a coach: An unintegrated wound activates, and an undertow starts pulling you into some negative vortex. The fear of getting "swallowed up" keeps a person from welcoming such experiences. So, we make sure that the coaching conversation is filled with positive resources, to help the client "be with without becoming" a negative experience.

This is a major reason we list transforming obstacles as the fifth of the 6 steps. We want to start with resources and positive connections into which the CRASH experiences can be welcomed. While obstacles often show up long before the fifth step, we still recognize that our first connection is to the resources that can welcome and support the obstacles in a positive human community.

With COACH resources and connections, we carefully work with the wounded self. We anticipate that CRASH may happen at any moment, and we're ready to shift attention—sometimes in mid-sentence—to a resource. By thinking of transformation as the re-weaving of a disconnected part into the mosaic of their COACH field, good things happen.

With COACH resources and connections you can open options to welcome archetypal energies that are trying to express something.

Relational Focusing

There's one more method that we want to touch upon that we call *relational focusing*. It is influenced by Eugene Gendlin's (1978) work at the University of Chicago. Gendlin found that sustainable creative change occurred only when a person's verbal mind was connected with somatic resonance in their body. In other words, disconnected thinking or speaking has little power. But words touching the body, that's a winning combination. This is why we often use what in generative coaching we call the ***cognitive/somatic crossover question***:

> *As you say (or think) that, take a few moments to sense how that is represented in your body.*

We're looking here for what Gendlin came to call *felt sense*. It's not a muscle-locked emotion, it's the resonance of the quantum river flowing through the somatic center, each moment an ever-changing revelation of subtle knowing. Gendlin developed an approach called *focusing*, where attunement to this *felt sense* is used to unfold generative solutions. In this process, the individual mind is in partnership with the ancestral wisdom mind. We need this deeper intelligence, just as it needs us.

In Gendlin's version, the focus was just on the client's somatic felt sense. In generative coaching, we find even deeper results by a *relational focusing* on the somatic centers of both client and coach. You are not "merging" with your client; on the contrary, having both client and coach focus on their own centers while joined in limbic resonance creates much better differentiation, like two performance artists fulfilling the generative equation of $1 + 1 = 3$.

Just as important, you're going "straight to the source." Milton Erickson used to say that *neurosis in the inability to speak directly*. In other words, when you're stuck in a problem state, your cognitive maps are not congruently representing your deeper somatic truths. To activate creative power, the two levels need to be aligned. This is what we're looking to do with relational centering. We move attention from the verbal statements "upstairs" to what's being touched "downstairs" in the somatic centers, and then see if we can get "the elevators moving up and down."

There are many ways to do relational focusing. Sometimes I suggest the following to a client as an exercise in somatic centering and listening. We take a few moments to settle in and settle down, then I explain that I'll start with my eyes closed. Instead of trying to understand the words, I'll just listen and feel what gets touched in my center, along with any images that pop up. This is a powerful learning for many people: That when they really want to understand something, they can close their eyes and just "listen to the music play." Most people have never been given permission or encouragement to do this, at great cost.

As the client talks, I touch my hand to whatever somatic center (of mine) that begins to resonate. This becomes an integral part of my professional mind; it feels like some additional presence has joined me, as I imagine anyone in a creative state feels. I'll gently open my eyes and while staying connected to my center, ask the client to pause and sense and connect to their felt sense. Once they find it, I'll ask them to return to talking, *but only in a way that allows continued resonance with their center*. When you cannot feel your center, stop thinking or doing until you can. Again, conscious performance is only creative when connected to a somatic felt sense.

This direct connection to felt sense provides understanding that you would have never imagined if the conversation just stayed "upstairs." It's especially helpful when you feel something is happening that you just can't put your finger on. I often use it when listening to a client talk about their situation, to check if what I'm hearing "upstairs" is matching what I'm sensing "downstairs." Or sometimes it seems like a technique *should* be having some effect, based on your understanding of things, but it's not. Other times, the client will walk out of the office so excited about apparently making some deep change, but then nothing happens afterwards. Or just in conversation, you get some strange feeling, like fog descending, or shimmering images or faces, or changes in temperature or light.

All these are suggesting that something "behind the scenes" is active. Remember, this is a good thing: The activation of "outside the ego box" experiences are signs that the creative unconscious is attempting to bring in resources to meet some challenge. The caveat is, human presence needs to positively meet these energies in order for them to be resources. Relational focusing can really help in this regard. It allows you to drop underneath the "social chit-chat" and directly sense what's trying to come through.

What comes is often quite surprising, quite unrelated to what's happening upstairs. It may seem like a person is touching something important, but you feel strangely untouched. Or as they talk about some seemingly innocuous topic, you feel a deep sadness or a numbness. Sometimes somatic focusing brings strange images—recent sessions included images of a house burning down, an ancient tree in a desert, a baby crying, and a woman breathing fire.

You never want to regard these felt senses or symbolic images as literal or "true." Gendlin described them as symbols that carry multiple, contradictory meanings, a number of which cannot be made explicit. Again, this is the language of creative consciousness. The important thing is sensing "something is trying to wake up," and to share your experience with clients in a way that they can sense their own. This begins a relational focusing conversation where each word, each sound, each movement is felt as rippling and shimmering through one's awareness. That's fertile ground for deep change.

An Illustrative Example

Let's look at a case example that weaves many of the techniques we've touched upon so far in this chapter. Diana worked as a HR manger for a tech firm. She was 48 and married with two children. In the opening session, she talked about how she loved her work, which focused on helping young "budding star" executives with "communication issues." She stated that sometimes she would get "overwhelmed with stress" during conversations with them, and become self-critical afterwards. Her goal was to do well in such conversations.

Diana was very positive, charming, and intelligent. She smiled almost constantly and spoke very fast. Not surprisingly, it was hard for to get sustained deep connections to a COACH state. She could identify a number of positive states of well-being—for example, walking on the beach, and cooking—and positive resources, such as her two beloved wolfhounds and her women's community. But when I coached her to settle into any one of them, it was hard for her to fully relax.

Similarly, she was not very clear on her positive intention. She really wanted to do well with her clients but...she would often suddenly CRASH during interviews. It seemed clear that as she talked about work, some stress would activate in her body, but it was difficult for her to verbally talk about it. This suggested that using the verbal channel to connect to the somatic stuck places might not be the best path, so I suggested we do a little experiment in relational focusing, to which she agreed.

S: *Diana, as you talk about your goal, what I notice is your shoulders get tense, and you start smiling and speaking faster. How about you? What do you notice?*

D: *Yes. I start feeling kind of uptight... I just start to feel overwhelmed... but I don't know what it's about.*

S: *Well, I'd like to suggest we do a little experiment. It's something called **somatic focusing**. I'll ask you to talk about your goal for a few minutes, and I'll settle down with my eyes closed, just to get a feel for what that might be touching, in me but also for you. Ok for you?*

(Diane nods head.)

S: *Great. So let's take a few moments... for each of us to just slow down... breathe...* (voice gets gentle, resonant) *... and let's find our own version of what I've been calling a COACH state... Centered... open... aware... connected... hospitable... You might remember your dogs... walking on the beach... and I'll use my own way... And then, when you're ready, you can open your eyes...* (Diana opens her eyes.) *... just go ahead and talk about your goal here today... and as you talk, I'm just going be listening in a centered way to what gets touched in me.* (Takes a deep breath and closes his eyes)

D: (Diana talks again about her goal. Steve's eyes are closed... after a few moments, he touches one hand to his heart area. After another 20 seconds or so, staying centered and absorbed, he brings a clenched hand to his belly area. He nods his head slowly and continues to listen.)

S: (Opens eyes) *And Diana, let's just pause... and breathe and sense what's going on in the body. I noticed first how kind-hearted and charming you are as a professional, in your social presentation...* (points gently to Diana's face) *... and then as I listened to that, I felt a sort of over-vulnerable fear in my chest...* (touches heart gently) *... and then* (smiles and clenches fist in front of his belly) *... I felt this cold dark presence down here... interesting, huh? I wonder what you noticed in your body as you talked about the goal?*

D: *Well, I can relate to what you're saying about my "niceness." People often say that about me... and they comment on how I always seem to be smiling...*

S: *Yes, I see that niceness and caring and positive presence in your face...that's good to see and feel... and how about your heart and chest?* (Steve touches his heart, points to Diana's.)

D: *Well, that's what's kind of confusing. Sometimes at work, especially with those young whiz kids who are a bit full of themselves... I start feeling this anxiety...* (touches her chest) *... and I tell myself to just relax... but it doesn't seem to work...*

S: (Nodding his head). *Yeah, I see that... So, as you try to bring that "niceness" to your clients* (points gently to her head) *... something happens here* (points to heart) *... and there's some really intense anxiety...*

D: (Nods, looks perplexed) ...

S: (Touches hand to this chest). *Yeah, I felt that... really great that this deeper resource begins to activate...* (smiles) *... Let's slow down and take a few deep breaths. And I'd like to say to that place of tension in your chest: **Welcome!*** (Smiles, gently waves). ***Welcome!***

D: (Diana smiles, nods, relaxes)

S: *And just notice that as I say that, what happens to that feeling in your chest?*

D: *The energy comes back to my feet, I can feel my feet, and the breathing is deeper, and that (indicates chest) is not a storm anymore. It shifts from feeling really cold to warm...*

S: *Isn't that interesting? That when you can bring positive support and connection to that presence in your chest, it begins to relax and your warmth returns?*

D: (Relaxes, breathes deeper, nods.)

S: *So, it sounds like, so far, we've identified two different parts of you that activate in those professional conversations. You've got your professional skills and caring "upstairs" (points to D's face) ... that's good to know... and when you hit these challenges, then a second "part of you," the vulnerability in the heart, starts to activate. That's good to know, too.*

D: (Nods). *I think it's there all the time* (touches heart) *... For whatever reason, it just freezes sometimes and it gets overwhelming...*

S: *Yeah... that resource in your heart is always there... and sometimes, like maybe when the conversation starts getting into some weird dynamics... it begins to go into lock-down...* (touches heart) *...*

D: (Nods, looks soft.)

S: *I'm sure that makes sense. And then, if I'm sensing correctly, at some point a third part of you begins to activate* (touches closed fist to his belly) *... as I listened, I felt this intense fierce red fire... something or someone that you wouldn't want to mess with... in your belly.* (smiles) *and to that presence, I want to also say:*

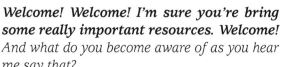

Welcome! Welcome! I'm sure you're bring some really important resources. Welcome! *And what do you become aware of as you hear me say that?*

D: *I start to get irritable.* (Hands and jaw clench, voice almost like a growl.)

S: *Wow, that's interesting! (Both laugh a bit.) Don't you find that interesting?* (Steve growls as if angry.) *Welcome!*

D: *It's interesting, but I don't find it pleasant.*

S: *I see that. I feel that. So, to that presence in you (points to belly), I again want to say:* **welcome***. It's really interesting that every time you start feeling in some way unsafe, that presence suddenly pops up…*

D: *Yeah, I think you're right…*

S: *So, some "bullshit detector" and "protector" activates.* (waves). ***Hi!***

So, I would love to support you in seeing what kind of new relationship you can have to that part of you that's getting irritable. And by the way, I just want to share that as I was tuning to that belly, I saw a few images… there was a house burning down, and dog barking on a leash… not sure what those might mean… but curious if you notice any images as you connect to that "irritating" part?

D: *Well, that's very strange that you saw that image of the house burning down. Apparently, my grandmother burned her house down when she was a teenager.*

S: *Wow… what happened with her?*

D: *She ended up catatonic, in a hospital.*

S: *Wow... so you're really tapping into something pretty deep inside. Well, fire can destroy things, it can also provide a lot of light and passion... So again, I'd like to say to that place deep in your belly,* **welcome!** *Welcome into our conversation.* (He indicates the circular space again. Diana nods.) *I'm sure you're bringing something really, really important. And just, as you hear me say that, what do you notice happen?* (He indicates his chest.)

D: *This place starts (points to her chest) to relax. And for a moment, I felt like you talked to me. It calmed down.*

S: *Yeah.*

D: *It's like I feel understood...*

S: *Yes, that's exactly what we're trying to do. We're looking to touch that part of your soul... with human eyes of kindness and understanding. Because if I am understanding correctly, you're saying that when you really need to be in a good state at work, you have three different parts of you: (1) the natural charm and skill of your professional self* (points to head) *... (2) the tremendous vulnerability and delicate feeling of your heart... And (3) the intense fire and protective fierceness of your belly mind.*

When those three parts are positively connected, you've got an unbeatable creative team. But if any of them gets shut out or negatively attacked, you're gonna end up with a lot of troubles. Make sense?

D: *Yes, very much so...*

Humanizing negative experiences allows you to make new choices on how to express what is really important to you.

We then continued to tune to each of the parts, positively welcoming them into COACH states, and then moved through processes of feeling an alignment between the head, heart, and belly minds. Diana moved through a series of deep integrative experiences, as she felt and integrated the positive roots of each part. I then invited her to stand up and walk through timelines of feeling one connection, then the next, then the next. Through this process, each part was emphasized as a core resource that activated whenever she needed that resource; that sometimes a negative history conditioned it into a CRASH form that elicited negative relationships; and how her positive COACH responses could ensure that each part became an integral member of her generative self.

Transforming negative experiences

1) SET AN INTENTION

2) FIND THE "VOICES/ FEELINGS" YOU EXPERIENCE AS NEGATIVE

3) OFFER THEM HUMAN PRESENCE TO TRANSFORM...

4) ...INTO RESOURCES

Bring human presence to your negative experiences, listen to their message
and transform them into ressources

Summary

In step 5, we welcome the unavoidable, integral presence of major negative experiences and behaviors in every part of life. Without these challenges, learning and creative development would literally not be possible. The dual-level model sees each obstacle as representing a core archetypal resource, activated from the collective mind in response to some challenge. At its base level, the pattern has equal potential to be positive or negative, depending on the relationship. When you engage a core challenge in a CRASH state, it appears as a negative problem; but when you can shift to a COACH state, the same pattern can be transformed into a positive resource.

This understand allows us to positively welcome the significant negative experiences that seem to be blocking a client's creative path. Generative coaching offers many ways to transform these obstacles into creative resources, based on skillfully bringing positive human presence—through a COACH state, humanizing language, connecting to resources, and giving place. We also saw how sometimes we need to move from "upstairs" verbal thinking to "downstairs" relational sensing to connect with presences hidden in the conversational "hypnosis."

Very importantly, we accept not only the inevitable presence of obstacles, but look forward to creatively connecting with them. We might say that a core statement we encounter in coaching is:

I want to create X BUT (the obstacle) Y interferes.

In GC, we shift that to:

As I go to create X, (the resource) Y shows up to help.

This core representational shift allows the game-changing move from fight/flight/freeze/flow to the creative flow that allows new solutions to develop.

I will not die an unlived life
I will not live in fear
of falling or catching fire.
I choose to inhabit my days,
to allow my living to open me,
to make me less afraid,
more accessible,
to loosen my heart
until it becomes a wing,
a torch, a promise.
I choose to risk my significance;
to live so that which came to me as seed
goes to the next as blossom
and that which came to me as blossom,
goes on as fruit.

~ Dawna Markova

Chapter 7

Step 6
Practices for Deepening
and Sustaining the Change

One of the most important findings in psychotherapy research over the past 60 years is that all approaches work about the same, with around a 60% success rate (Miller, Hubble, Chow, and Seidel, 2013). (This is counter-intuitive to practitioners, who usually think their approach is vastly superior!) We're confident that this finding holds equally for coaching, as well as related "improvement" approaches. But while there's not much outcome differences in approaches, there are significant differences in practitioners: Some get consistently better results than others.

It turns out that there are three major differences between average and generative practitioners. First, the high performers get vastly more feedback from clients, at every level. The sessions truly unfold collaboratively, with the client being included at every step. Second, successful coaches admit failures more often and more readily; they realize everything they offer is a "suggestion," and they really don't know what's best for the client. They find the techniques that don't work are as helpful as those that do, each providing feedback about how to shape the session to fit the unique patterns of the client. Third, high performing practitioners are committed to their ongoing development. They practice consistently, for both personal and professional development, always looking to "extend their edge." This not only allows them to be fully engaged, but also provides a great model for clients to do the same.

This sixth step of GC is about ensuring that whatever happens in the session, translates into creative realization in the world. Sustainable change comes from staying connected to the core patterns of the client. We want to focus in this chapter on three ways we do that:

1. Feedback at all phases of the work

2. Homework assignements

3. Daily practices

1. Feedback, Feedback, Feedback

When I (SG) work with clients, I often have an inner mantra: *Touch me, teach me, touch me, teach me*. I want to be touched by the unique spirit of the client and be taught how to best support its organic growth. The central importance of deep listening cannot be overemphasized. One of the most astonishing things I hear from most people is how as children they were always told what to do, and rarely asked about what they wanted. This "father knows best" mentality carries over in most social institutions and is a main way that generative spirit is damned, and sustainable growth doomed.

There are two English terms for learning: *instruction*, which means "to pack in"; and *education*, which means "to draw out what's already there." *Instruction* is the dominant tradition. In generative coaching, we're looking to replace it with spirit-honoring *education*. One can never have advanced knowledge about the exact way that creative change will develop. Our only real hope is to extend an invitation and then pay very close attention to the feedback—verbal and nonverbal,

TOUCH ME,
TEACH ME,
TOUCH ME,
TEACH ME...

big and small, positive and negative. With the four relational mantras, we're attuning to *something is waking up* and then *welcoming* whatever arises, especially uninvited experiences. And when we're using a technique, we're not so much expecting that it will succeed, but are curious about how it will stimulate the client's own organic intelligence. By receiving whatever happens with aikido-like presence and respect, changes organically unfold from within the client, which is what most supports sustainability.

The table below outlines the different types of feedback, both formal and informal, that generative coaches pursue before, during, and after sessions. **Before the first session**, clients are asked to fill out **Appendices A and B** (as briefly described in Chapter 1.) Appendix A invites clients to share general information related to the work—their familial and professional backgrounds, their previous experience with coaching or related activities, goals, and resources, etc. The coach reads this before the session, typically touches upon it in the first session, and periodically refers to it in subsequent sessions.

Getting Feedback from the Client	

Pre-session
  a. Office policies
  b. Bio info (Appendix A)
  c. Specific goals: 6 GC "performance elements" (Appendix B)
	End of Session
	  a. Brief feedback form (Appendix C)
	  b. Brief discussion/ "feed forward" with homework tasks
	  c. (optional) GC 6-elements feedback

During Session
  a. Non-verbal resonance
  b. Verbal/non-verbal "crossover question"
  c. Frequent "small chunk" checking (is this right?)
	Post-session
	  a. GC 6-element feedback (Appendix D)
	  b. Beginning of next session: reflections/feedback/setting goal for present

Appendix B concentrates on the 6 steps of the GC *performance holon*. This is the primary focus of GC: we're looking to identify and make creative use of the client's performance holon. When each dimension is resonantly held in a positive, interconnected way, sustainable generative change is possible. The pre-session form provides a baseline assessment. It suggests what resources and patterns a client has, as well as weaknesses that need to be strengthened. Post-session use (Appendix D) allows us to see where changes have occurred, and what needs further attention. We are also coaching clients to use this *performance holon* information to guide and inform their self-generative processes.

During the sessions, the coach is intensely attuned to the client, noting and being guided by every subtle response. Remember, words only become generative when they somatically resonate, so the generative coach is noting the somatic responses of both self and client. Many times, we ask the *cognitive/somatic "crossover question"*:

When you say (or hear or think) that, what happens in your body?

This question is intended equally for the client and the coach. This applies not only to the client's somatic mind, but the coach's as well.

As has been illustrated, sometimes the coach says:

As I listen to that, I notice that my body starts to feel X. What do you notice happening in your body?

As we discussed in the last chapter, this type of "relational focusing" illuminates the relation of the conversation to a person's deeper identity. Sometimes the resonance is positive – such as a warm relaxation or kind-hearted openness – indicating a COACH connection. Sometimes the resonance is negative – such as a clenched tension or a strange energetic field – suggesting a disconnected CRASH part that needs integration. The CRASH and COACH responses equally reveal the core identity parts needed for a transformational conversation. The best way to attune to them is continuous nonverbal connection. Sometimes it's a negative resonance, or even a cold numb feeling, indicating a CRASH dissociation. Beggars can't be choosy: we need every emotional resonance to prepare a healing meal.

A final type of feedback is gained by simple questions of the sort:

> *If I understand you correctly, you are saying X. Did I get that right? Is there anything else you think is important to add?*

Such questions are asked throughout the session and provide crucial feedback. This doesn't require that the understandings of the client and coach always match. Differences are just as helpful as agreements, as long as the coach realizes that holding "both at the same time" is often very generative.

At the end of the session, feedback from the client is very helpful. This can be done informally, but also through the brief written form shown in Appendix C. Research shows that just having the client fill out such a form improves outcomes, *even if the coach doesn't read it*, presumably because it invites and supports clients in thinking about the session as belonging to them (see Miller and Hubble, 2011). And when coaches read such feedback, an additional boost in outcome is gained!

Of course, feedback is also received after the session, and before the next session (Appendix D). In all of this, remember the core GC premise that creativity is always a conversation. Generativity is not inside either the individual client or individual coach, it's in the feedback-resonant connection between them. That's where the magic happens!

As we've been saying, the coaching session creates *possibilities*; actual change only happens afterwards, when the person reenters their ordinary life. Thus, homework is an integral bridge for the transition. The following illustrates the basic way we do this, as collaboratively as possible.

> *So, we did this work and we were exploring this issue. You identified a sense of what you want and you identified some of the difficulties. This is a starting point. If you were to take two or three things that you think are important to be able to carry over and to continue in your real life... what would be at the top of the list in terms of things to accomplish? For example:*
>
> 1. *What do you need to do?*
>
> 2. *Who do you need to talk to? About what? When?*
>
> 3. *What skills do you need to work on, what knowledge do you need to find out?*
>
> 4. *What commitments do you need to make?*

2. Goal-oriented homework

1. *What needs to be done to realize the goal?*

2. *Commitment to a few homework assignments*

3. *Keep records and return to coaching sessions*

4. *Using responses (or lack of) as major feedback for further work*

From that conversation, clients are asked to identify and commit to a few things to accomplish. The coach looks to ensure that they are clear, do-able, relevant, and time-committed. Clients are asked to write the goals down and keep daily diaries of what they did in regard to the goals, the outcomes, and any revisions.

At the next session, the diaries are reviewed and discussed. Predictably, many things happen in regard to the homework assignments. Sometimes clients complete them, things go pretty well, a lot is learned. But other times, homework is not completed or even started, which is tremendously important information. It tells you that something in the client's system is not being included in the conversation. Here's another place where using the 6-part *performance holon* is helpful. You can check:

1. **COACH field:** Was the client able to access the positive self-connections needed for generative action?

2. **Positive Intention:** Is the goal clear? Is there sufficient motivation?

3. **Generative state:** Was the client able to access the three positive connections (center/ intention/ resources)?

4. **Action steps:** Was there a clear representational map/commitment of specific actions to take?

5. **Obstacles:** What hidden parts/CRASH experiences/ fears are blocking creative action?

6. **Daily practices:** Is the client practicing self-care and self-connection regularly, to allow a resilient sense of well-being to develop?

In many ways, this is where the work really begins. It's not difficult to have a session where the client leaves with a sense of, "*That was great! Now my problems are completely gone... Now I'll live happily ever after!*" When the fantasy hits the post-session reality, it becomes clear what needs to happen for sustainable change.

Types of Responses to Post-session Commitments

1. *Things went well, new experiences and elaborations.*

2. *Didn't do commitments.*

   - *Check motivation*

   - *Need to prioritize commitment and arrange time*

   - *"Chunk down" commitments to do-able size*

   - *Identify what else needs to be done first*

   - *Identify and work with hidden objections/obstacles*

   - *Commitment to daily focus on goals*

3. *When doing commitment, CRASH occurs and derails process*

4. *Focus on positive outcomes of doing commitments, and negative outcomes of not doing. (Positive and negative motivation.)*

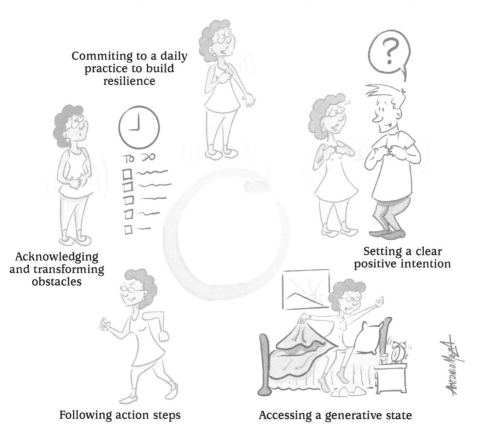

Commiting to a daily practice to build resilience

Acknowledging and transforming obstacles

Setting a clear positive intention

Following action steps

Accessing a generative state

Sometimes it's a matter of clients reorganizing their lives to make room for themselves. Most of us have created lives dominated by our responsibilities to everybody but ourselves. This becomes clear when we can't find the time to do our own work. So "not having time" for the committed homework allows a really important conversation about reorganizing one's priorities to include yourself.

In *GC Volume 1* we shared the example of how, on every plane trip, the flight attendants point out that, in case of an emergenty, oxygen masks will drop down in front of you. They then invariably instruct you to put your mask on first before trying to help others. We make a similar point with our clients. We need to give "oxygen" to ourselves first in order to be able to be of service to others.

**As soon as we commit to a course of action, "objections"
appear as a CRASH state.**

Often, unintegrated experiences CRASH into a person's creative path. For one client, their commitment to self-care activated tremendous conflict in her family, as her unconscious role of the "caretaker" was threatened. For another client interested in professional development, old voices (*You have no right to speak! You're an idiot, nobody is interested in what you have to say!*) issued "death threats" that froze her into inaction. Again, such experiences are the norm, not the exception. To reiterate, these CRASH energies carry the deepest soul energies of a person, and so their presence is really good news. Helping clients develop an intelligent, compassionate relationship to these inevitable obstacles is one of the most practical goals.

As with all GC processes, these conversations are not just verbal, you're especially looking at the verbal/nonverbal congruency. The *performance holon* emphasizes the generative self as a family of multiple, contradictory selves. So, it should not be surprising that after the person's "front self" has committed to a course of action, other parts jump into the conversation as "objections" or "sabotages." We welcome such events as core parts of the generative integration process.

Then we can welcome that "failure" as one of our generative practices.

This positive welcoming of "failure" is one of the most generative practices we can develop. Inevitably there is a big gap between our *ideal self* and what actually happens. We fall short, we dissociate again, we fall back into old patterns. *This is a universal, unbridgeable gap.* Many of us are conditioned to pummel ourselves with self-hatred and punishment at such points, which is what makes it a problem. Welcoming such "other than ego" responses as integral members of the creative team is a game-changer.

3. Daily Practices

The other major part of Step 6 is developing a commitment to daily practices. We ask clients to make a daily commitment—30 to 45 minutes—to practices devoted to self-care and self-connection. Often clients say:

> Oh, that's a great idea. But I don't have time. Can't you see what an important busy person I am? But when I have time, I'll do it.

We say:

> Illegal answer. Life is never, never, never going to give you time for yourself. You have to take it. If you don't take it, you're not going to be able to make sustainable generative change. On the other hand, we guarantee you that when you take it, you'll have more time for everything else in your life.

We are both exceptionally busy people, and have learned that without daily practices, we'd probably be hospitalized. We usually recommend a balance between *quieting/centering* and *skill development* or *rehearsal practices*.

In the absence of a "daily practice" our busy life takes over and we never "find time"

Quieting/Centering Practices

Contemporary life locks most of us in an underlying CRASH state. We're tethered to the machine world of computer/television/internet/texting – existing in a perpetual state of "do-do." The concept of psychological stress was developed in the 1930's by a young Montreal medical resident, Hans Selye (1956). Making the rounds in the hospital, being educated in the *differential diagnosis* model of identifying signs of specific illnesses, Selye still couldn't help but notice that all the long-term patients (and staff!) looked sick! This suggested some shared base for chronic illness, and he coined the term *stress* (and then *chronic stress*) to describe what we call an underlying CRASH state. It is now generally recognized that stress (or chronic CRASH) blocks healing and well-being, and so we regard daily COACH practices as non-negotiable commitments for creative living.

As we discussed in *GC1*, most clients already have such practices, and it's often more a matter of having them engage in them regularly. Remember the general question to identify such practices:

When you really need to de-stress and come back home to your self, what works best for you?

A person might say: *gardening, cooking, walking in nature, yoga or meditation, reading, music or reading...* Such experiences satisfy a psychobiological need to go into some sort of flow state. If we don't have positive ways to meet this need, we are very prone to addictions that try to do without our human presence.

Yoga, meditation, gardening, reconnecting to nature... are just a few examples of quieting/centering practices you can adopt.

Some clients have a very difficult time fully letting go or relaxing, so sometimes the quieting/centering experiences need to first be developed within the session. The generative coach always has their "antennae" tuned to any signs of positive resonance—e.g., in the casual mention of a great book or movie recently experienced, the reminiscing of a favorite childhood activity, the softening when a friend or special person is mentioned. These are all portals into the quantum resonance of a COACH state, and we blow on them like faint embers, slowly building up the warmth and illuminative light of a COACH fire.

Once a client is at least periodically connecting to COACH experiences, they can be used for both positive and negative motivation. That is, you use the positive experiences to point out what life can be like, and what creative performances and personal relationships can be like when grounded in COACH. You then can compare that to what happens when a person lives in CRASH—the self-hatred, the unhappiness, lack of creative development, and so forth. We want to build up a clear comparison, so you know not only the person you can be when practicing self-care, but the person you become when you don't. This "double awareness" is especially clarifying and motivating, because you see just how much is at stake, and how you have the power to be "the difference that makes the difference."

When I am in COACH state my imagination is a creative resource, but when I am in CRASH then it is a source of anxiety (note of the illustrator).

Skill Development and Mental Rehearsal Practices

Complementary to the quieting practices are those that focus on skill development and mental rehearsals. It can be helpful to practice any of the GC techniques practiced in sessions—for example, *the three positive connections, the three archetypal energies, the community of resources, touching others with your intention, somatic modeling of goal/obstacle dances, etc.* It can be especially helpful in doing slow, *Taichi-like* dances around long-standing CRASH patterns—for example, collapsing under criticism, responding to stress with addiction responses, feeling helpless and overwhelmed. We've seen how we can connect to the underlying deep structure and positive intention of such patterns via somatic modeling, and then transform them into resources via COACH versions of the same somatic models.

We never assume that the negative patterns will disappear forever. We also assure clients that the Chinese principle of *impermanence* applies, especially to positive experiences. In recognizing that CRASH experiences will visit us for the rest of our lives, we realize that a positive relationship to them is our most practical approach. We come to appreciate them as representing the best ways we had to deal with overwhelming circumstances, and now value them as "red flags" signaling a need to return back home to COACH. By practicing ways to welcome CRASH response, and slide them into COACH connections, we make friends with the enemy and stop the war.

As with the quieting practices, we ask clients to select rehearsal/skill practices best for them. A very popular choice is a daily timeline practice, where the client visualizes a timeline for that day's schedule, then slowly walks through it in a generative way. The person might do 10-15 minutes of quieting, then stand up and do a slow movement through the six steps. For each step below, the person steps forward into that step:

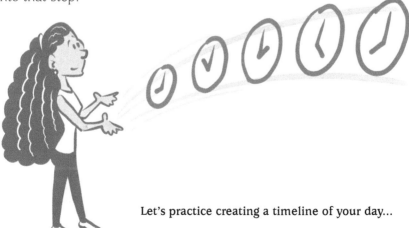

Let's practice creating a timeline of your day...

Step 1 (COACH field): And now I start with a COACH connection to myself... *(somatic model)*... and to the larger world... *(somatic model, pause)* ... and as I open to the world, I see the day in front of me... (somatic model, pause).

FLOW

Step 2 (Positive intention): And as I see the day in front of me, I sense: *What is it that I really want to bring forward into the world today?* (somatic model, pause) ... Make statement... pause to absorb... (somatic model, perhaps repeated several times).

Step 3 (Generative state): And as I walk on this path today, I remember the three connections: *center* (somatic model) ... *intention* (somatic model)... *resources* (somatic model) ... And some of the resources I especially want to stay connected to are...(name resources, represent somatically)...

Step 4 (Action steps): And through this day, I commit to small steps forward... moving my intention into the world... (somatic model) .step by step... this movement... *this breath...* bit by bit... always coming back to COACH... (somatic models). intention...resources... action steps (somatic model) ...

Step 5: And as I move forward, there's going to be some tough spots today... conversations that trigger me (somatic model) ... and I will find a way to reconnect and find COACH responses to myself and the situation... (a few moments for somatic modeling) ... people that trigger me (slow somatic model in COACH) ..., and I will find a way to reconnect and find COACH responses to myself and the situation... (a few moments for somatic modeling) ... there will be outcomes that disappoint me (somatic model with COACH) ... and I will find a way to reconnect and find COACH responses to myself and the situation... (a few moments for somatic modeling) ... soooo many CRASH to COACH experiences to look forward to today... (somatic model).

Step 6: (Integration/Future orientation). And in moving through the day in this way, I find myself at the end of the day... (somatic model, pause) ... tired, but happy... (somatic model) ... An appreciation of a job well done, a sincere and complete effort given... (somatic model) ... and so a moment to integrate... (somatic model) ... express gratitude... (somatic model) ... get some rest (somatic model) ... and say to the world: *I'll be back!*

As with all GC processes, we are curious about what happens in each of these processes, creatively utilizing each response as positive "feedback and feedforward" information.

A Few Questions

L: *What if one of the goals is:* What I want to create in my life is more discipline?

S: *Well, we'd first want to get more context specific: In what area of your life would more discipline really make a difference for you?*

L: *Well, I try to have discipline in all areas. And sometimes I'm really good, I can hold it for three months. And then something happens, and I can't anymore…*

S: *(Laughs). Well, two things. First, we'd really want to get more context specific, because that's where all the important dynamics are. Your creative patterns only activate in connection with something in the world.*

Second, if I'm hearing correctly, you're saying something like: Damn, I can white-knuckle it for three months, and then the polarity kicks in. Three months would be like a world record for staying so one-sided! (They both laugh.)

L: *You mean, that's why I feel so exhausted and burnt out?*

S: *Yes. You didn't say that, but you could predict it. Remember Jung's term of **enantiodromia**: everything not only contains its opposite, but like the yin/yang symbol, everything is always in the process of turning into its opposite.*

That one-sided focus means you're holding the intention from a CRASH state. You can see that in the rigid somatic state when a person is trying to create "forced discipline". It'd be helpful to invite the other side into the conversation: What would happen if you didn't force yourself into discipline? What does "no discipline" look like?

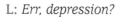

L: *Err, depression?*

S: *Yeah, so here's where somatic models come in really handy. We could ask: What would be your somatic model of discipline?*

(L., laughing slightly, puts one hand forward like a karate chop. Body very rigid)

S: *And then the opposite: If you weren't disciplined, what would your somatic model be?*

(L., eyes closed, tongue out, lolls her head sideways.)

S: *Great. That one actually looks more fun. I take it there was a rule about being playful and silly when you were a kid?*

L: *Yes, it was very strict.*

S: *So, a relaxed body meant... ?*

L: *I somatize a lot – I get things that prevent me from working. I just had tendonitis, and I had sinusitis, so that's – my body reacts like that. Yeah.*

S: *Well, you can hear the two conflicting parts there: I get so sick I can't work. But that state of "not working" has so much pain and tension...*

L: *That feels really right on...*

S: *So, the practice would be untangling the two sides—disciplined working and deep surrender and not-doing—then practicing COACH versions of those two sides. I know that's different from the starting point, but I hope it makes sense how we got here.*

L: *Yeah, and it really does.*

S: *Remember, every pattern—discipline, play, relaxation—has a COACH and a CRASH version. We're always making sure that the COACH context is present, otherwise everything we do ends in CRASH.*

L: *Thank you.*

S: *You're welcome! One more question?*

K: *I asked my client to keep a daily diary of her activities, and it kind of backfired. She ended up staying up for hours, feeling more and more anxious about trying to understand why she was having difficulty. Any suggestions?*

S: *Yes. First step,* relax... *Remember, when your client goes into CRASH, your mirror neurons ensure that you do, too. So, feel the CRASH, center, drop into COACH...and then find a way to authentically say:* That's interesting, I'm sure that makes sense. *I'm serious.*

Client got homework from her coach... to write a diary. But she felt anxious.

The basic pattern seems to be that when she had a writing assignment, she went into CRASH and got carried away by it. In that disturbance is the client's deepest creative spirit. You just need to open a COACH space and settle down. Sometimes with anxiety, it's especially challenging, because they have these whirling dervish skills of taking the tiniest, most innocuous detail and quickly spinning into an anxiety hypnosis. So, you drop into your center, not tracking or trying to interrupt their verbal mind, and feel a connection to the person underneath the verbal

First thing to do is "relax" and welcome the CRASH.

"LET'S ADD OTHER POSSIBILITIES"

Then get authentically curious about how to best support your client.

tornado. When your center touches their center, you just limbically tune to that. They'll start feeling you, they'll get a little curious. Then you might find gently say something like: Maybe we should add some other possibilities to writing assignments. *With kind-hearted, gentle playfulness, you reflect back that it really touches some deep CRASH response, and you want to invite that part into the conversation. Then you'll probably want to, very gently, get curious about how it might be playful or feel gentle... something complementary to their cognitive understanding. Remember what we've been saying: when you make suggestions or have clients do assignments, you never know what it will touch. But as Milton Erickson would say:* I'm very curious to find out. *And then the important thing: Whatever comes up in the conversation is likely a part of the* **performance holon** *of* **generative change**. *You just need to figure out a way to sympathetically welcome it into the conversation. Then finding a COACH connection to that part or those parts becomes an integral part of the session work and the homework.*

Make sense?

K: *It wouldn't have six months ago, but now it makes a lot of sense. Thanks!*

S: *You're welcome.*

Summary

Everything we do in a session is preparation for what a person does in their ordinary life. The sessions have no value greater than the shifts that a person experiences afterwards. So, we're seeing generative coaching as a conversation between two worlds. We're taking a step back from performing in the world to open a safe place for generative connection and repatterning, then following that over the bridge to actual changes in the outer reality.

The work inside the session benefits from detaching from all fixed maps and conditioned responses, to swim in a conversational ocean of infinite possibilities. But as a session begins to move towards completion, we begin a sort of reversal, focusing on how the transformations of the sessions can fit into the "valences and vicissitudes" of a client's everyday living. To be sure, we're hoping that there are deep changes in the underlying quality of a client's connections – with their body, their emotions, their thinking, their relational connections with others – such that fixations become fluid, obstacles open resources, and somatic movement and feeling is more like a dance than a locked machine. Throughout the session, we're future orienting to new possibilities in their real life, hoping to nurture a consciousness that senses every challenge point in terms of infinite possible pathways of response.

We're emphasizing life as first and foremost a performance art, requiring daily mindbody training. To live on this "learning edge" that moves you ever further into life, takes a lot of practice. It's hard work being spontaneous! The focus of Step 6—especially the "twin towers" of commitment to goal achievement and daily mindbody practices—is what truly translates the dream into a reality beyond words. It's good to know that this is possible, and great to realize that generative coaching is a tradition to support it. What more could one possibly ask?

Four Quartets

We must be still and still moving
Into another intensity
For a further union, a deeper communion
Through the dark cold and the empty desolation,
The wave cry, the wind cry, the vast waters
Of the petrel and the porpoise. In my end is my beginning.

– T.S. Elliot

Chapter 8

Practicing the Deep Structure: The 6 Steps in a Timed Session

As we begin to bring closure to this second volume, let us remember the base of the generative coaching model: Consciousness is creating reality through multiple levels and living beings. It is a great breathing ocean, giving birth to endless waves of living forms. Humans are a special type of wave, with the evolutionary gift of being able to represent potential realities and then organize to realize them. This makes creativity the core property of human consciousness.

Generative change sees human creativity as a "performance holon" that contains 6 basic dimensions: maps of (1) present state, (2) desired state, (3) *images of achievement* (action plans for achieving the desired state,) (4) resources to support the journey, (5) obstacles to transform and integrate, and most importantly, (6) the creative field to hold and creatively use each dimension. We see that intentional action is often done with *neuromuscular lock*, which freezes the creative field and locks the representation maps into separated, feedback-insensitive parts. This freezing is compounded by stress, and results in the inability to live in the present moment and move forward in a positive way.

This inability to creatively live one's potential is an integral part of what brings people to generative coaching. GC works with this with our 6-step model:

1. Open a COACH field

2. Set a positive intention

3. Develop a generative state

4. Take action

5. Transform obstacles

6. Practices to sustain and deepen the change

These first two volumes of the work hopefully give you a working sense of what this means at a practical level and, at this point, you have a feel for the different levels of the 6-step level. Each step is a principle that can be used in infinite ways, a number of which emerge from the unique conversational connections in a given session.

At a basic level, the 6 Steps are used as a timeline sequence, each step unfolding from the previous, with prototype methods for each step. But at the more advanced level that we're touching upon in this second volume, we see each step containing all the other steps, with each step having multiple possible expressions, and the unfolding sequence as well.

For example, a generative goal/intention implicitly carries the COACH field inside of it, allowing it to be sensed as a sparkling jewel with many facets. Without the COACH field, the goal would be a rigid fixed representation to be imposed on the world, a situation that would not produce sustainable change. We also see the obstacles as implicitly contained in the goal: There is no positive intention unless there's a perceived negative obstacle blocking it. Also, each goal implicitly carries a set of understandings, often unconscious, about what the end state looks like and what needs to be done to reach it.

We assume that whatever the client is bringing into the coaching conversation, contains many fixed representational maps that don't fit the challenges of the present goal. So we first shift the primary state to one of **open presence** in which each representation is *fluid, feedback sensitive*, and *interconnected*. Like a piece of performance art, we then enjoy the beauty of an unfolding creative process that moves in ways that have never been seen before. This is the core of generative change.

Somewhat paradoxically, we always end each training module with a simple version of the 6 steps, in the form of a timed sequence. The session is 35 minutes long, with 5 minutes for each of the 6 steps, plus an additional 5 minutes for processing and feedback. This not only allows an integrative process of seeing how all the pieces practiced in the module fit together, but also illuminates a simple **deep structure** rhythm of just staying connected to the core principles of each step. Practicing this really helps you get the model deep in your bones, so that you are not locked into any fixed surface structures so that, for every session, you can feel *a river of consciousness* runs through it.

So, let's now turn to an example of that timed process. This is a session that Steve did with a gentleman named Leon at the end of a GC training module in St. Petersburg, Russia. Off stage there is a moderator calling out the 5-minute intervals.

(Leon comes up onto the stage. He takes a seat, and S and L shake hands.)

S: *Welcome. On this last day, let's see if we can do a good, sincere, helpful piece of work. I'd love to support you in any way I can.*

Step 1. Open the COACH Field

S: *Like in any process, it's good to set up a place to center, focus, really tune in...* (Leon closes eyes, begins to breathe more deeply) *... Begin in the most natural, helpful way to... pull your attention together, let go of all the ego-pleasing stuff... and see if you can connect to what you really, really want to be doing in your life that'd be great to focus on here... Then sensing how you can find the proper state within yourself, relaxed, connected deeply to your core* (Leon opens eyes) *... a positive determination, good concentration, good relaxation.*

Is there any way that is really helpful for you to tune in to that COACH state?

L: *I remember the lineage of my ancestors. I think of my grandfather, and he brings this groundedness to me.*

S: *Did you know him?*

L: *No, we just have his medals of honor.*

S: *Awesome. Notice where you feel that connection to the courage, the honor, the great legacy that your grandfather lived and passed down... Where do you feel that the most, in your body? That love for your grandfather... that sense of honor and pride?*

L: (Slowly moves hands over his thighs, then from his belly down to the knees, then from his chest to his knees.)

S: (Sensing that something is not quite balanced, shifts attention to a different part of the identity system.) *Do you have kids, Leon?*

L: Yes, three.

S: How old?

L: 12, 20 and 21.

S: Wow, that's generative. You heard that story of the Israeli prime Minister, Golda Meir? A reporter said, "As the Prime Minister, when you need to talk to somebody, who do you talk to?"

She replied, "That's easy. I talk to my grandmother and my granddaughter. My grandmother, who's no longer living, and my granddaughter, who's not yet born."

Leon (laughs a bit): *Yes, that's great.*

Step 2. Set Intention/Goal

S: So, sort of tuning to that lineage (S slowly mirrors the movement Leon made, moving his palms from his forehead slowly down) *… Your grandfather, yourself, your kids, your grandkids at some point…* (brings palms together near forehead and moves them like Leon was moving his hands) *What would you say you really, really want to live more of in the world or create more in your life?*

L: I have a lot of playfulness in me, I love this about myself. But sometimes, I just cannot express it or don't find a place for it around. I want to express this playfulness more (he leans forward and looks at Steve, very seriously), *but in a suitable way.*

S: Great. Okay. (Leon's microphone falls down and he bows down to pick it up. Steve responds playfully by saying: ***I thought that was your wallet falling out of your pocket onto the ground. I was going to distract you***) *(points in the opposite direction).* (Laughter on the stage.) (**Note:** This was to begin to bring a bit more playfulness into the conversation.)

But that sense of really wanting to bring more playfulness ~ in which part of your life would that be really great and might make your grandfather very proud? And your kids would be like, "Wow, check dad out!"

L: (Laughs a bit): *In my work life, in work, to make my work more elegant, more precise, like playing the violin, showing this playfulness in a really precise and refined way.*

(**Note** that these words are not exactly connoting playfulness, but rather the opposite.)

S: *What do you do?*

L: *Psychotherapy.*

S: *What kind of psychotherapy do you practice?*

L: *It's something that combines brief therapy and hypnotherapy and Ericksonian hypnosis.*

S: *Cool. So, if you let a somatic model of being playful* (throws arms out, leans forward, looking intensely) *… ~ what would be a somatic model?*

L: (Leans forward, looks at Steve.) *Here it is.* (Extends his hands to Steve, as if formally giving a gift.) (Steve looks at him like a child, pretends to receive something.)

S: *But you look more earnest there than playful.* (Mirrors Leon.)

L: *Yes.*

S: (Makes a face and silly movement, Leon laughs): *What would be totally non-earnest, goofy?*

L: (Laughing, makes a loose circular gesture forward with one hand.)

S: *Okay!*

L: (Moves his hand like swinging a lasso over his head, opens arms wide.)

S: *Great. And I'd like to say to that* (opens arms) *presence, "Welcome!"* (Makes gestures in different directions) (A number of audience members, deeply connected from previous days, spontaneously also express this. **Welcome! Welcome! Welcome!**)

(Looks out into the audience.) *Wow... I wonder what it would have been like to have this group as your family when you were a child?*

L: *Yes, that would have been nice...*

Step 3. Develop a Generative State

(Moderator's voice calls out next step.)

S: *Are you hearing voices? (Laughter.)*

L: (Apparently referring to his internal dialogue). *They didn't think that the structure would be playful...*

S: (Playfully) *Are you hearing a voice now?*

L: *I hear lots of voices.*

S: *And what was the voice saying?* (Stuffy voice) *"Now you must go to Step 3. – The manual says..."* (S utilizes the serious moderator, who is giving the formal time signals for each step.)

L: *Unfortunately, yes.* (Leon looks a bit sad, suggesting his state being dominated by critical voices.). *But I also have some voices that want to play, to go further with what we're doing now.*

S: *So, if you were to step into one of them and respond to that serious schoolteacher over there,* (In a styffy voice, pretending to look at a manual)*: "Now, Leon, pay attention."* (Folds arms in the Russian school manner. Leon chuckles a bit, looks up, sighs.) *Did you do this in school?*

L: *At first, yes. (Folds his arms.)*

S: *So, when the teacher says, "Leon, pay attention, go to Step 3,"* (crosses arms again), *what would one of the goofy ones say?* (Smiles.)

L: (Laughs, makes a rude hand gesture of defiance to the imaginary presence.)

S: *I think your grandfather just woke up, hm?* (Senses that the defiant expression activated his grandfather's presence in the field and feeds it back.)

L:(Looks a bit surprised, wide-eyed, then nods with tears in his eyes.)

S: (Gently) *Now he can begin to rest in eternal peace, seeing that you are beginning the healing.*

L: (Touches chest)*: Yes, that's close, I feel it close.* (Looks deeply touched with a mixture of a little boy filled with love, loneliness, confusion…)

S: *(Sensing that the grandfather carries deep emotional wounding, asks very gently) I hope it's okay to ask: How did your grandfather die?*

L: *He decided to take his own life – it was a suicide.*

S: *Hmmmm… (Nods, breathes, absorbs the sadness.)*

(**Note:** The grandfather, who was a venerated war hero, killed himself. Imagine the effect that would have on young Leonid, especially on his playfulness.)

L: *And I didn't know him.*

S: *How old was he?*

L: *40.*

S: *Oh. He got the medals for the Second World War?*

L: *Yes, for the Second World War. He was a really joyful person, he brought back two accordions and his medals, and he actually had completed the journey to Berlin – he marched all the way with the Russian army to the final victory in Berlin.* (Note: Leonid did not know his grandfather directly, only this is part of the story: the joyful and courageous war hero who killed himself.)

S: *Oh. Wow. And then, how long after the war did he take his own life?*

L: (Rubs his hands around his knees) *I haven't thought much about it. Maybe ten, twenty years? He created a family, he lived further, and there were also other women, which interfered with him continuing his life path.* (Note: Again, this is part of the family story.)

S: *Hm. Hm* (nods.) *So, am I correct in sensing that your intnetion of "I want to live a good life, but I really want to be able to bring a spirit of play" is partly* (puts a hand on his heart) *to honor the spirit of your grandfather? It sounds like he* (Leon puts a hand on his heart) *took on so much suffering* (Leon rubs his heart slowly.) *that he was never able to quite recover.* (Steve brings out his arms wide.)

Step 4. Take Action

L: *Speaking about him, he went away unrealized, he died not having achieved his goals, not being realized. It was a great feast at the place where he lived while he was living.*

S: *Was he your mother or father's father?*

L: *My mom's.*

S: *How did that affect her? What kind of person was she? Was she serious, depressed?*

(S is looking to fill in the family story mosaic, particularly curious about transgenerational wounds that may be active.)

L: *Determined. Individual. And I think she was also not fully realized. He told her, "Ira, you will have everything," and then he died.* (Sighs.)

S: *Mm... I'm sensing that that really* (indicates heart area) *hit you hard* (puts hand on his heart) *as a kid and was sort of confusing.*

L: (Nods): *It just comes together now, as we talk. Up until now, I didn't face it consciously in my head.*

S: *And then your mom and your dad struggled* (brings two fists together): *Was your dad a pretty serious guy, or playful?*

L: *He was tough, strict and really tough, and sometimes violent. Sometimes cruel.*

S: *Mmmm...*

L: *It was an embodiment of his manhood, of being a man, but it was really, really tough.*

S: (Nods): *... So, you became a psychotherapist.* (Smiles).

L: *Yes. He wanted me to be a priest.* (They laugh.) *But I went for therapy.*

S: *Thank God. It would have to be long-term therapy if you'd said 'yes' to his order to become a priest.* (Both laugh a little more.)

So, with all that pain and suffering in the family, and as much love as you feel for your family, it sounds like – how old are you?

L: *46.*

S: *It sounds like, if I'm hearing correctly, you've kind of gotten to a point where you're sensing: To really express my love for my family without … getting lost in the way that my mom did in her way, and my dad did in his way, I need to be loving, serious, AND playful.* (Smiles, opens arms).

L: *Yes, different from them.*

(All this suggests the transgenerational field of violence and unfulfilled dreams, which makes it hard for Leon to fulfill his intention to live playfully as a way of healing himself and his family wounds.)

Step 5. Transform Obstacles

S: *Yeah. So maybe we can stand up.*

(They stand up, Leon stands in a location representing the present.)

(**Note:** When an emotional state seems locked or heavy, it often helps to shift posture, especially by standing and moving a bit.)

S: *So, as you stand here with this sense of: Here I am at 46, I can feel running through me from my past this amazing courage and integrity of my grandfather, and the recognition that he received, and how he held it so much inside that he ended up taking his life.*

L: (Nods, his hand touching his heart.)

S: *Somehow, you've carried that all of your life.* (Leon nods.) *... And then feeling both your mom and your dad, how much love you felt connecting to each of them* (Leon breathes in and out deeply), *how they eventually were held back. ...*

And now, it's sort of (Steve gestures from behind Leon towards him) *passed on to you* (Leon nods.) *in terms of how do you carry the seriousness, the trauma history, the wanting*

*to honor your family and be a good person? …
And then something inside of you suggesting
it's probably every day of your life you're going
to have to consciously choose to be playful*
(opens arms with some playfulness) *precisely*
because *life is so serious.*

L: (Nods.)

S: *The only way to do it without feeling suicidal
or angry or depressed is in the face of the
seriousness:* (opens arms, steps into future
place and stands there) **Play.** *That's what I
heard you saying – am I hearing correctly?*

L: (Nods.) *Yes, you have understood very well…*

S: *So maybe we can just do that process: Each
day I step into, I can feel the pain (Leon puts
hand on his body), the loss, the violence, … and*
because *of that,* (Steve opens arms playfully) *I
play. Maybe we can just do that as a movement*
(steps forward, opens arms diagonally).

L: (Chuckles, opens his arms, steps forward,
clicks his fingers, moving forward.)

S: *And then to pause* (playfully lifts up hands
flamenco-like) *and to feel; I do this partly because
I carry the pain of my family in me (opens arms).*

L: (Opens arms wide.)

S: *I feel it, I don't run away from it.* (Steve
opens arms like holding something, then
opens them upward and wide.)

L: (Nodding, opens arms wider. Steve begins
playful arm movements. Leon laughs, begins
to dance on the spot, moving his arms.)

S: *So, you can let me see your pain.*

L: (Becomes serious, nods, touches his heart
for a moment.)

S: (Makes rude hand signal, begins to make playful faces like a young child as a way to begin to integrate the intention of **playfulness** with the obstacle of **trauma-based seriousness.**)

Step 6. Practices to Deepen the Changes

(Both move on the spot, laughing.)

L: *I hear my grandfather's voice saying to me: You rascal!*

S: *And how do you respond to the serious taskmaster* (pointing to the time-keeping moderator) *that says: Pay attention and follow the rules!* (Folds arms rigidly in the Russian school-child manner) *You're supposed to be on Step 6 now!*

L: (Opens his arms towards the moderator, as if inviting her to play) *Come, sweet woman, please join us!* (Laughter).

S: (Waves at moderator, moves very playfully, as if a young defiant Leon): *I am paying attention! This is how I pay attention.* (Steve folds his arms and begins Russian dance movements, sings a bit.)

L: (Still laughing, makes relaxed dance movements.

(Audience is cheering, laughing…)

S: (Serious, gentle): *And what do you imagine your kids doing right now? "Check out dad!" What do you think your kids think about that?*

L: (Places his hand on his heart, contemplating and sensing.) *The oldest one thinks: Dad is crazy… My daughter, she kind of keeps distance – she* (gestures far away) *studies to be a doctor, so she's like* (shows very serious face) *… but the little one, he just joins.*

S: *Well. I put toenail polish on my toenails twice. I was at this supervision retreat, and I walked by and there were 4 or 5 women sitting on the ground, painting their toenails. And I said, I am so jealous! I mean, don't you think it's one of the great things women get to do* (mimes putting on lipstick and makeup, being radiant)? *You know, as guys, we* (looks down at his body, stands stiff, head back, "no" gesture).

(Leon laughs, audience laughter.)

And one of the women picked up a polish— purple color—and offered it to me. (Steve then models panic and horror, to everybody's laughter). **Me? Be sensual? Not be serious?**

And the woman said: **Well, how about you just try it with one toenail?** (Steve models being curious, pondering...) *It was the summertime, and I was wearing flip-flops, so I sat down with them and painted my big toenail purple... radiant, outrageous purple! I came back home, I think my daughter was 15 at the time, and she saw it and said:* **Daaaaddddd, that is so gross. You're embarrassing me.** (Steve models horror of his daughter.)

I said: **Ok, ok, ok, I'll take it off.** *But once you get a taste, you want more. So maybe 6-7 years later, I did two toenails. I came back home, I think Zoe was 22 by then, and she said:* **Cool, dad, why didn't you do all your toes?**

(Steve and Leon laugh together at sharing "father stories" of a daughter at first not supporting her father's playfulness.)

S: *Leon, you look great when you laugh... It's a beautiful way, I think, to carry the sadness of life with dignity and defiance. I think that's where the Irish and the Russians share so much*

L: (Closes his eyes, touches his heart, breathes in and out deeply, as if integrating something very deep.)

S: *And you know, the feeling of love that you have so deeply. And with that, bearing the suffering and love for your family… and precisely because of that, committing to playfulness as a balm for the soul.*

L: (Nods, closes eyes.)

S: *That's a nice balance, hm?* (Leon nods.) *So may you always remember, when you feel that pain, that the way that we bring that pain into some loving way for ourselves and for everything, everybody we love* (makes peace signs, then one rude and one "peace" hand signal) *is we **insist** on playing.*

(Looks out at the audience, which has been so supportive and present). *Any thing you want to say to the community here?*

L: (Chuckles, turns to the audience, opens his arms.)

(Applause.)

S: *Awesome. Okay if we stop?*

L: *Yes, it's very good.*

S: *Good luck. I really felt you willing and able to go to a good core place. And you probably could see in that work what we were talking about: how important the balance of tenderness, fierceness and playfulness is.*

(To the audience). *So, you can see in this session, the stated intention was pretty simple and straightforward: **I want to be more playful in my life, especially in my work.** You could also see that when he communicated that intention, his nonverbal and verbal behavior were anything but playful. So, operating with that attitude that **I'm sure this makes sense**, it didn't take much to discover that his family history didn't really support playfulness—the war traumas, the suicides, divorce, abusive father, and so forth.*

*We're interested in how all these different parts—the longing for playfulness, the loyalty, suffering, family resources—can integrate together. We welcomed the pain and suffering, and defined them as support for the playfulness. **When each part of the system is recognized, welcomed, and included, sustainable generative change is possible.** The 6-step model helps us to identify those parts, but a non-linear utilization is what ultimately allows the generative integration.*

Leon, thanks so much for sharing a deep piece of your journey. I know I received a lot from it in terms of my own personal journey of healing and development, and I suspect many if not most of the other people in the room did as well. (Audience nods their heads and give a standing ovation to Leon.)

Practicing the Deep Structure

1) COACH STATE AND INTENTION

2) ACKNOWLEDGE CRASH/OBSTACLES WHENEVER THEY APPEAR

3) TRANSFORM OBSTACLES BY ACKNOWLEDGING COMPLEMENTARITIES

4) ESTABLISH
PRACTICES TO CREATE
SUSTAINABLE CHANGE

Summary

Generative Coaching is a process of ***disciplined flow***, a method for awakening deep creativity. This creative consciousness has two levels: (1) an ***unbroken wholeness*** of the unity of life-past, present, and future, and (2) a partitioning and "mapping of the territory" into many parts. When the connection to the wholeness is felt, then the integration of the parts allows a deep transformation of lasting import. This is the general process of all performance art, and we situate generative coaching within that domain.

Opening a COACH field for coach, client, and the relationship is the necessary first condition, then a skillful connection of the parts into an integrated mosaic is what transforms the representational filters that create experience. The 6-step model details the core dimensions involved in the process. As they are differentiated and generatively actualized, the potential for miracles opens. This is, for us, the true *structure of magic*.

Conclusion

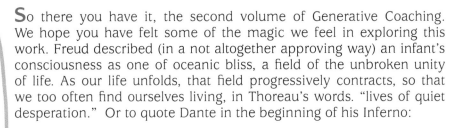

So there you have it, the second volume of Generative Coaching. We hope you have felt some of the magic we feel in exploring this work. Freud described (in a not altogether approving way) an infant's consciousness as one of oceanic bliss, a field of the unbroken unity of life. As our life unfolds, that field progressively contracts, so that we too often find ourselves living, in Thoreau's words. "lives of quiet desperation." Or to quote Dante in the beginning of his Inferno:

Here I am in my middle years, having wholly lost my way.

The signs abound, but the spirit is forever unwounded and unwoundable. This is shown by both the passion for creative development and communities, as well as the suffering incurred when we fall short of realizing them. In generative coaching, we see sparks of life in both suffering and joy, and look to slowly fan those embers into creative fires that warm and light the way.

What seems clear is that there is no fixed formula or fundamental text to lead us, but there are many paths that creative consciousness can walk that have heart and soul, as well as creative success. We hope that this second volume gives you a deeper sense of how you can support that in yourself and others. We're half way through the series, we look forward to bringing the next two volumes to you soon.

All the best!

Steve and Robert

Appendix A

Client Information Template

NOTE: THIS IS MEANT AS A SAMPLE FORM. YOUR INTAKE FORMS SHOULD CONFORM TO ANY LAWS/PRINCIPLES OF YOUR REGION AND/OR PROFESSIONAL LICENSE.

Name: ____

Address: ____
Street City, State, Zip Code

Phone(s): ____
Home Work

____
Cell/Pager Fax

E-Mail:

Date of birth: ________________ Place: ______________________

Social Security#: ________________ Drivers License#: ________________

Current Occupation - # of years: ______________________________

Past Employment - # of years in each: ______________________

____

____

Education: ____

____

Past/Present religious affiliation: ______________________________

____

Marital status/committed relationship history:_____

_____

_____

Parents and siblings:
For each, please list name, age, marital status, present location and occupation:

_____

_____

_____

_____

_____

Children (if any)
Please give name(s) and age(s):

_____

_____

_____

Session goal(s):

_____

_____

_____

Previous therapy/coaching experience-

_____

_____

_____

History of drug/alcohol abuse or significant traumas in your self and/or
family member(s):

_____

_____

_____

Other notable key events in your life:

_____

_____

_____

_____

_____

_____

Please list any medications that you are currently taking:

_____

_____

_____

Hobbies/Interests:

_____

_____

_____

Skills/Strengths:

_____

_____

_____

Who may I thank for this referral?

_____

_____

_____

Generative Coaching Pre-session Form

In Generative Coaching, we find there are six important areas for sustainable creativity: (1) getting into a positive (COACH) state; (2) connecting to positive goals; (3) developing and maintaining creative performance states; (4) outlining timeline action plans; (5) overcoming obstacles; and (6) establishing daily practices. Please write down your best answers to these six elements, to help both you and me in the work.

1. **Your ways of positive self-connection.** Please list at least several of your best ways to find positive self-connection with yourself (e.g., walking in nature, music, pets, breathing/meditation, etc.)

2. **Positive goals/intention.** What I would most like to create/experience/achieve in my life is _____. Give at least several positive answers, that is, experiences you would want to have. Be as specific as possible in terms of with whom; in what context (personal, professional, self). Identify a brief (5 words or less) verbal statement, plus color image(s), plus a somatic movement to represent the goal/intention.

3. **Creative state.** Your thinking/feeling/acting is only as good as your underlying state. Identify resources you have (people, places, historical or spiritual beings, ancestors, teachers) that allow you to access a positive state. Also identify any ways you cultivate a positive performance state.

4. **Plans/timelines.** What changes do you think you need to make to achieve your goal? What actions do you need to take? What connections need to be established?

5. **Obstacles.** What emotional states do you think block you from achieving your goals? Which relationships do you think you need to change/repair? Other inner or outer conditions that you think prevent you from achieving your positive goals?

6. **Daily practices/homework:** Do you have any daily practices for self-attunement? If so, please list, including how much daily time you give for them. Also, ideas for adding daily practices?

Generative Coaching Session Brief Feedback Form

Any positives outcomes of our work depend on much honest feedback. Regarding this session, please rate the following, using a 1 to 10 scale (1-3 = not at all, or not much; 4-7 = somewhat but not fully; and 8-10 = very much, or completely). Feel free to write any any additional feedback.

1. I felt heard, understood, and respected.	
2. We focused on what I really wanted/needed to focus on.	
3. The approach is a good fit for me.	
4. There was something missing in the session for me.	
5. I feel more confident about achieving my stated goals.	
6. I feel more open and creative regarding my negative states.	
7. My overall rating of the session.	
8. Other....Please offer any additional feedback.	

Appendix D

Generative Coaching Post-Session Form

Now that we've done some work, let's revisit your connection to what we call the 6 elements of Generative Change. Please reflect upon and write down your present relationship to the 6 elements.

1. **Your ways of positive self-connection.** Note any changes in: ease, frequency, stability, or way of developing your positive self-states.

2. **Positive goals/intention.** Have your goals/intention changed? On a scale of 1-10 scale, how much have you achieved your goals? What's more to do?

3. **Creative state.** In terms of developing a positive performance state where you can feel/think/and act creatively, how much are you able to do that now? What are your best ways? What do you need to work on here?

4. **Plans/timelines.** How much of clear timeline have you been able to develop? What small steps are still needed? Are you keeping track of specific goals and daily achievement?

5. **Obstacles.** How much of a shift have you experienced regarding the negative states that have previously overwhelmed you? Biggest challenges in terms of facing, transforming, and creatively engaging with the negative obstacles?

6. **Daily practices/homework:** What daily practices do you have, how frequently are you practicing them, and what is your daily "average level" of well-being?

Many types of feedback

1. Pre-session

   a. Office policies

   b. Bio info

   c. Specific goals: 6 GC "performance elements"

2. During session

   a. nonverbal resonance

   b. verbal/nonverbal "crossover question"

   c. frequent "small chunk" checking (is this right?)

3. End of session

   a. Brief Feedback form

   b. Brief discussion/"feed forward" with homework tasks

   c. (optional) GC 6-elements feedback

4. Post-session:

   a. GC 6 –elements feedback

   b. Beginning of next session: Relections/feedback/ setting goal for present

Bibliography

* Bateson, G. (1972). *Steps to an Ecology of Mind.* New York: Ballantine Books.

* Csíkszentmihályi, M. (1991). *Flow: The psychology of optimal experience,* New York: Harper Perennial.

* Csíkszentmihályi, M. (1996). *Creativity: Flow and the Psychology of Discovery and Invention.* New York: Harper Perennial.

* Dilts, R. (2003). *From Coach to Awakener,* Santa Cruz: Dilts Strategy Group.

* Dilts, R. (2015-2017). *Success Factor Modeling, Volumes I-III,* Santa Cruz: Dilts Strategy Group.

* Dilts, R. (1990). Changing Belief Systems With NLP, Santa Cruz: Dilts Strategy Group.

* Dilts, R., & Gilligan, S.G. (2021). *Generative Coaching, Volume 1.* Santa Cruz, CA: The International Association for Generative Change.

* Duncan, B., Miller, S., Wampold, B., & Hubble, M. (eds.) (2009). *The Heart and Soul of Change: Delivering What Works.* Washington, D.C.: APA Press.

* Eliot, Thomas Stearns. (1943). *Four Quartets.* New York: Harcourt Brace.

* Erickson, M. H. (1980). *The Collected Papers of Milton H. Erickson;* New York: Irvington Publishers Inc.

* Gebser, Jean. (1949). *The Ever-Present Origin: Part One: Foundations of the Aperspectival World.* (Translated by J. Keckeis). Stuttgart, Germany: Deutsche Verlags-Anstalt

* Gendlin, E. (1978). *Focusing,* New York: Bantam.

* Gilligan, S. (2012). *Generative Trance: The experience of creative flow,* Carmathen, Wales: Crown House Books.

* Gilligan, S. (1997). *The courage to love: Principles and Practices of Self Relations Psychotherapy,* New York: Norton Professional Books.

*   Gilligan, S. (1987). *Therapeutic Trances: The cooperation principle in Ericksonian hypnotherapy.* New York: Brunner/ Mazel.

*   Gilligan, S., & Dilts, R. (2009), *The Hero's Journey: A voyage of self-discovery,* Carmathen, Wales: Crown House Books.

*   Goswami, A. (1993). *The Self-Aware Universe: How Consciousness Creates the World,* New York: Tarcher/Putnam.

*   Haley, J. (1973). *Uncommon Therapy: The Psychiatric Techniques of Milton H. Erickson,* M.D., New York: W. W. Norton & Co.

*   Joye, Shelli. (2017). *Tuning the Mind: Geometries of Consciousness - Holonomic Brain Theory and The Implicate Order.* Viola, CA: Viola Institute.

*   Joye, Shelli. (2017). *The Little Book of Consciousness: Pribram's Holonomic Brain Theory and Bohm's Implicate Order.* Viola, CA: Viola Institute.

*   Joye, Shelli. (2019). *Sub-Quantum Consciousness: A Geometry of Consciousness Based Upon the Work of Karl Pribram, David Bohm, and Pierre Teilhard De Chardin.* Viola, CA: Viola Institute

*   Koestler, A. (1964). *The Act of Creation: A study of the conscious and unconscious in science and art,* New York: Macmillan

*   László, Ervin. (2006). *Science and the Re-Enchantment of the Cosmos: The Rise of the Integral Vision of Reality.* Rochester, VT: Inner Traditions.

*   Laszlo, Ervin. (2007). *Science and the Akashic Field: An Integral Theory of Everything.* Rochester, VT: Inner Traditions.

*   Levine, P. (2010). *In an unspoken voice: How the body releases trauma and restores goodness,* Berkeley, CA: North Atlantic Books.

*   McGilchrist, I. (2009). *The Master and His Emissary. The Divided Brain and the Making of the Western World,* New Haven: Yale University Press.

*   Miller, S.D., & Hubble, M.A. (2011). *The road to mastery.* The Psychotherapy Networker, 35(2), 22-31, 60.

* Miller, S.D., Hubble, M.A., & Duncan,B.L. (2007). *Super-shrinks: Learning from the Fields Most Effective Practitioners.* Psychotherapy Networker, 31, 6, 36-45, 57.

* Miller, S.D., Hubble, M.A., Chow, D.L., & Seidel, J.A. (2013). *The outcome of psychotherapy: Yesterday, Today, and Tomorrow.* Psychotherapy, 50(1), 88-97.

* O'Donohue, John. (1997). *Anam Cara: A book of Celtic wisdom.* New York: HarperCollins.

* Osbon, D. (1991). *Reflections on the Art of Living; A Joseph Campbell Companion.* New York: HarperCollins.

* Pribram, K. (1971). *Languages of the Brain: Experimental paradoxes and principles in neuropsychology.* Englewood Cliffs, NJ: Prentice Hall.

* Pribram, K. (2013). *The form within: My point of view.* Wetport, CT: Prospecta Press.

* Sapolsky, R. (1988). *Why Zebras Don't Get Ulcers: An Updated Guide To Stress, Stress Related Diseases, and Coping,* New York: W. H. Freeman.

* Selye, H. (1956). *The Stress of Life.* New York: McGraw Hill.

* Wallas, G. (1926). *The art of thought.* New York: Harcourt, Brace, and Co.

* Wangyal, Tenzin. (2002) H*ealing with Form, Energy, and Light: The Five Elements in Tibetan Shamanism, Tantra, and Dzogchen.* Itacha, NY: Snow Lion Publications.

* Watzlawick, P., Weakland, J., & Fisch, R. (1974). *Change: Principles of problem formation and problem resolution.* New York: Norton.

* Wilber, K. (2001). *A Brief History of Everything.* Boston: Shambhala.

* Yeshe, Thubten. (1987). *Introduction to Tantra: The transformation of desire.* Boston: Wisdom Publications.

About the Authors

Robert B. Dilts

Robert B. Dilts has had a global reputation as a leading coach, behavioral skills trainer and business consultant since the late 1970s. A major developer and expert in the field of Neuro-Linguistic Programming (NLP), Robert has provided coaching, consulting and training throughout the world to a wide variety of individuals and organizations.

Together with his late brother John, Robert pioneered the principles and techniques of Success Factor Modeling™ and has authored numerous books and articles about how they may be applied to enhance leadership, creativity, communication and team development. In addition to Robert's three volume series on *Success Factor Modeling*, his book *Visionary Leadership Skills* draws from his extensive study of historical and corporate leaders to present the tools and skills necessary for "creating a world to which people want to belong." *Alpha Leadership: Tools for Business Leaders Who Want More From Life* (with Ann Deering and Julian Russell) captures and shares best practices of effective leadership, offering approaches to reduce stress and to promote satisfaction. *From Coach to Awakener* provides a road map and set of toolboxes for coaches to help clients reach goals on a number of different levels of learning and change. *The Hero's Journey: A Voyage of Self Discovery* (with Stephen Gilligan) is about how to reconnect with your deepest calling, transform limiting beliefs and habits and improve self-image.

Past corporate clients and sponsors include Apple Computer, Microsoft, Hewlett-Packard, IBM, Lucasfilms Ltd. and the State Railway of Italy. He has lectured extensively on coaching, leadership, innovation, collective intelligence, organizational learning and change management, making presentations and keynote addresses for The International Coaching Federation (ICF), HEC Paris, The United Nations, The World Health Organization, Harvard University and the International University of Monaco. In 1997 and 1998, Robert supervised the design of *Tools for Living*, the behavior management portion of the program used by Weight Watcher's International.

Robert was an associate professor at the ISVOR Fiat School of Management (the former corporate university of the Fiat Group) for more than fifteen years, helping to develop programs on leadership, innovation, values and systemic thinking. From 2001–2004 he served as chief scientist and Chairman of the Board for ISVOR DILTS Leadership Systems, a joint venture with ISVOR Fiat that delivered a wide range of innovative leadership development programs to corporations on a global scale.

A co-founder of Dilts Strategy Group, Robert was also founder and CEO of Behavioral Engineering, a company that developed computer software and hardware applications emphasizing behavioral change. Robert has a degree in Behavioral Technology from the University of California at Santa Cruz.

Stephen Gilligan, PhD

A seminal American psychologist specializing in creative change.

For over 40 years Dr. Gilligan has been writing, practicing therapy, coaching, and teaching all over the world. Considered one of the great hypnotherapists, his work has expanded far beyond the Ericksonian approach...

Stephen was one of the original NLP students at UC Santa Cruz; Milton Erickson and Gregory Bateson were his mentors. After receiving his psychology doctorate from Stanford University, he became one of the premier teachers and practitioners of Ericksonian hypnotherapy. This work unfolded into his original approaches of Self-Relations and Generative Self, and then further (in collaboration with Robert Dilts) into Generative Coaching. These different traditions have all been updated and integrated into the present Generative Change Work, which includes the applications of Generative Coaching, Generative Psychotherapy, Generative Trance, Hero's Journey, and Systemic Change work.

Stephen has taught in many cultures and countries over the past 30 years, and has published extensively. His books include *The Hero's Journey: A Voyage of Self Discovery* (co-authored with Robert Dilts), the classic *Therapeutic Trances, The Courage to Love, The Legacy of Erickson, Walking in Two Worlds* (with D. Simon), and *Generative Trance: The Experience of Creative Flow.* His forthcoming books are the *Generative Coaching* series (co-authored with Robert Dilts).

Antonio Meza is an architect of vision, supporting entrepreneurs and leaders around the world to communicate complex ideas in a simple and fun way through illustrations, cartoons, or through structuring presentations, books, or websites.

A native of Pachuca, Mexico, Antonio has a degree in Communication Sciences from Fundación Universidad de las Américas Puebla, a Masters degree in Film Studies from Université de Paris 3 –Sorbonne Nouvelle, a diploma in Cinema Scriptwriting from the General Society of Writers in Mexico (SOGEM), and a diploma in Documentary Films from France's École Nationale des Métiers de l'Image et du Son (La Fémis). He is also a Master Practitioner and a Trainer of Neuro-Linguistic Programming (NLP), certified in Generative Coaching and the three levels of the SFM system.

He worked in Mexico as a freelance filmmaker and participated in animated cartoons startups before moving to France where he works as a consultant, coach, and trainer, specializing in storytelling, creative thinking and collective intelligence.

Antonio is also an experienced public speaker member of Toastmasters International. In 2015 he was awarded best speaker at the International Speech Contest of District 59, covering South-West Europe, and reached the semifinals at international level.

He has illustrated 15 books including the 3 volumes of the *Success Factor Modeling* series with Robert Dilts, and now the *Generative Coaching* series with Robert Dilts and Stephen Gilligan.

He also uses his skills as a cartoonist and trainer to collaborate in seminars, conferences and brainstorming sessions as a graphic facilitator, and to produce animated videos to explain complex information in a clear and fun way.

Antonio lives in Paris with his wife Susanne, his daughter Luz Carmen and his cats *Ronja* and *Atreju*.

For more visit:

www.antoons.net

www.linkedin.com/in/antoniomeza/

Contact Antonio: hola@antoons.net

Milton Keynes UK
Ingram Content Group UK Ltd.
UKHW021256110624
444060UK00039B/923